TEXAS HOLD 'EM POKER

By the same author

Texas Hold 'Em Poker: Begin and Win
Bridge for Complete Beginners
The Right Way to Play Bridge
Control the Bidding

Uniform with this book

TEXAS HOLD 'EM POKER

WIN ONLINE

Paul Mendelson

RIGHT WAY

Constable & Robinson Ltd
3 The Lanchesters
162 Fulham Palace Road
London W6 9ER
www.right-way.co.uk
www.constablerobinson.com

This edition published by Right Way,
an imprint of Constable & Robinson, 2007

A copy of the British Library Cataloguing in Publication
Data is available from the British Library

ISBN: 978-0-7160-2186-5

Printed and bound in the EU

3 5 7 9 10 8 6 4

CONTENTS

INTRODUCTION

This is a book for poker players, experienced or comparatively new, who want to win playing online poker. It assumes some basic knowledge of the game, even if that has been gleaned only from modest home games and watching poker on television.

It also assumes that you are computer savvy – or you know someone who is: you have email, you use the Internet, perhaps you shop online. If you are, online poker will be easy for you. Although the game on which this book focuses is **No-Limit Texas Hold 'Em** – since it's the variation which is most widely played online, and still continues to grow in popularity worldwide – much of the guidance applies equally to other versions of the game.

Playing poker online is quick and simple; it is far less personally threatening than a live game. It is easier to re-buy chips, easier to cope with being shown a bluff, not really embarrassing if you make a foolish mistake. This is all positive, but it does lead to a certain looseness in the styles of most new or inexperienced online players. Ultimately, looseness leads to losses and that is why, for the expert, disciplined player, online poker is easier to beat than the live game.

Most significantly, it is easier to call online than in a live game. The mere act of clicking a button is so much easier than pushing forward a stack of chips and having to muck your cards when you see you've been beaten. Online, everything can happen smoothly and almost painlessly. Your opponent's superior cards are revealed; your cards get mucked, probably automatically. The blinds for the next hand are placed and the cards dealt even before anyone has had any time to react.

This tendency towards easy calling is a huge slippage from which many online players suffer. You want to eliminate such slippage yourself and watch your opponents' slippage heading in your direction!

Your assessment and knowledge of the players at your tables will be paramount, leading, as it will, to your table selection and the game in which you will pitch yourself.

I suspect that the majority of readers will already be playing online. For you, skip Chapter 1 and proceed immediately to Chapter 2. Before you do, however, you face a challenge: acknowledging that you are not doing as well as you should. Are you prepared to take a few steps backwards in order to learn the basics thoroughly?

To win online – and win steadily – is a simple skill to appreciate, but far harder to master and apply consistently. Whilst there are certainly hundreds of thousands, if not millions, of poor poker players online, exploiting your skill to record consistent profits is far harder than many imagine. Many experts think that as few as 5 per cent of online players make money from playing. That so few should be doing well is startling enough, but think more deeply and you will realise that this signifies that 95 per cent of players are winning very little, roughly breaking even (and breaking even doesn't really exist, except in the gambler's imagination) or losing. That last category is the one in which the vast majority of online players find themselves, even if only a small proportion actually admit it to themselves. Self-knowledge, as we will see, is a vital component of poker success, perhaps especially when playing online.

If you class yourself as an average, or just above average, player, then the chances are that you are actually losing, or winning only a little. This book will show you how to become truly above average and to record steady online winnings.

The good news for you, as a player wanting to improve – as we all should be – is that the online game is full of players with no interest in improving, and very little ability – and I'm talking a breathtaking lack of ability. To part them from their bankrolls, however, can sometimes prove more difficult than it might at first appear. There is a considerable medium- to long-term luck factor in Texas Hold 'Em, and loose games can often result in horrendous bad beats and frustrating sessions as players appear almost to gang up on you. To succeed, you require discernment in table choice, strategies and playing styles to counter each type of poker environment you find yourself inhabiting. This is what this book is about.

Your success at poker should not be based on how many pots you win, nor how much money you are winning. It is a game about decisions, and your level of ability (and, usually, your prosperity) will depend on how often you make the right decision, and avoid costly wrong decisions. Whilst much of the traditional psychology and tell-reading which makes the live game so fascinating, both to play and to observe, is missing from online poker, there are plenty of additional methods to discern what your opponents may be holding. The ability to provide false information and deduce accurate readings of your opponents is among the most important elements of online play.

Before we move on to the advice and information, you need to ask yourself some serious questions, the most important of which is this: do I really want to win money playing online poker?

Well, obviously!

Yet the vast majority of players demonstrate all the attributes of players who are determined not to be in profit at the end of the year. They don't do basic homework or preparation; they play when mentally, and sometimes physically, unfit; for the fun of it – the glamour, the excitement, the short-term adrenalin rush. They play to pass the time and escape the pressures of the real world. Poker seems like gambling where your skill can give you the edge, but there's no desire to hone those skills. These are perfectly good reasons to play poker – it is a game, after all, but, if you want to win, then to do so requires a little work.

Are you prepared for some gentle study? Are you happy to serve your apprenticeship? Can you take notes and keep records, not only of your opponents' actions but your own? Can you make those notes honestly? Can you concentrate hard for short periods? These are things a true card player can manage easily. The result will be that you will enjoy your poker more, and you will win money. So, ask yourself: do I really want to win?

One last word about life in poker rooms, online or live – when you go to Las Vegas, as a gambler, as a tourist, you must appreciate that the entire city is geared up for one ultimate purpose: to part you from as many of your cents and dollars as it can. It may dress it up, it may make you feel good (you may even win a little) but, ultimately, it wants every single dollar you have.

This is how you must approach a poker table. No matter how much fun you have, every good poker player will use every last trick up his sleeve to part you from your chips. If you are to succeed, you must resist these advances, and also be on constant watch for opportunities to set traps and bully your opponents out of their bankroll. If you have your mind on anything else – like having fun or showing off to your mates – don't expect to win.

And now, in the immortal words of the frustrated Poker Player – I'm gonna shut up and deal. Turn the page and good luck.

Paul Mendelson
London

1

THE ONLINE POKER WORLD

Getting Started

You are about to enter the online poker world. There, you will join a poker club – or clubs – get to be known as a member, recognised by your fellow players, and win and lose sums of money, perhaps small, perhaps huge. You are in control of how often you play, how much you risk, and how you conduct yourself. The more professionalism you can bring to your online persona from the outset, the less you will lose, the more you will win, and the better your reputation online will become. A strong reputation will earn you money just as surely as a well-timed bluff.

This is a brief outline of your first actions: each element will be discussed and explained in the forthcoming sections.

You select the poker site of your choice, download the software and check that the site offers you the games that you are looking for. Then, you sign-up as a member, choose a nickname for yourself and perhaps pick an avatar (a cartoon-like picture of the character you would like to be). Finally, you download some real money to your account online, and then, having investigated your options, you begin to play.

This process may take you a few minutes, or you may prefer to take it slowly and, over a period of days, become familiar with the idea of poker online.

Online Basics

Have the fastest, and most reliable, Internet connection you can afford. Get the proverbial four-year-old child to help you on any of the technical stuff if you are bamboozled by the online revolution.

And, make sure you are comfortable – you are going to be spending hours and hours and hours in that chair. One experienced player I know used his first six months' online winnings to buy a state-of-the-art office chair, a drinks fridge, and some funky lights for his study.

Try to ensure that your computer is out of the way of as many distractions as possible, especially children, your partner and/or house mates. This is business. Fun business, hopefully, but business all the same.

Picking a Poker Site

Pick your poker site by asking your friends and colleagues where they play; personal recommendation is the best route here. There are hundreds to choose from and it is not luck that just a handful have ended up being predominant.

The successful sites process financial matters efficiently and reliably, have 24-hour online and freephone telephone support. The layout will be user-friendly, easy to navigate, and the site will offer its players offers and promotions, such as free-to-enter tournaments (Freerolls), loyalty points for every cash hand you play, guaranteed and bonus payouts in big tournaments, as well as some more offbeat ideas like Bad Beat Jackpots and mystery winners.

Every online poker site takes a "Rake" – a small percentage of each pot. Almost all the leading sites take a similar sized rake (usually 5 per cent up to a maximum of a few dollars), and this issue should not, in terms of site selection, be one which overly concerns you.

You must ensure that your chosen site provides these two crucial features – all the top sites do:

- The facility to write notes on a virtual clipboard attached to each player – on every player you encounter – so that you can see those notes at any time.

- The facility to see immediately a complete record of any hand you have played at your table(s), so that you can study your own play as well as your opponents' action. Sometimes these records also reveal cards which may have been shown at the table but, for the sake of speed, were not.

These two features will provide you with a method of tracking play, rating your opponents and building up an information bank to help you to read your opposition. This makes these two facilities essential.

Mobile Gaming

This technology is just beginning to appear on the high street and, whilst currently the games available are focused on casino gaming, with built-in house edge, it will not be long before you can play against real opponents on your PDA or mobile phone. For the foreseeable future, my advice is to avoid these games completely. It will be almost impossible to concentrate using such a small screen, the response times may be very slow and connection problems may dog you. Although the software providers are reliable, site security and backup is likely to lag well behind the current industry standards.

Sign-Up Bonuses

When friends recommend a site to you, they should introduce you to the site – by submitting your name via their account – since, by doing so, they will receive a bonus and you should be given the best possible sign-up bonus also. Usually, they will email you a code to enter when you sign-up for the first time.

Do not select a site solely on the bonus that you receive

when first joining, as some sites offer misleadingly huge sums to lure you into joining them, and then don't release the promised riches unless you play 12 hours per day, every day.

However, that initial bonus can go a huge way to paying for your online poker education and for that reason is worth having. The reputable sites usually offer to double your initial deposit, up to a maximum amount (say, $600). That bonus is released slowly, but fairly, as you play on the site in the opening months of your membership. Check the terms of the bonus carefully before committing yourself to one particular site.

Legality

Just about every online activity is mired in some kind of legal challenge. At the time of writing, the United States has outlawed online gambling in any form, although there are plenty of US citizens still in the online poker rooms. Many of the poker sites (and online gambling sites) are based within judiciaries which monitor them beneficially and have no legislation preventing them. The UK is currently seeking to become a major player as a base for online gaming activities where, doubtless, they will be regulated efficiently and taxed.

There is no reason currently to think that your activity online, either gaming or playing poker, is illegal or restricted, other than in countries where general online restrictions and censorship exists, such as the United States.

Corruption and Collusion

Most online poker players will tell you that they doubt the integrity of online poker rooms. This belief stems from the short-term success of inexplicable, against-odds and expectation, and generally unbelievable play from some opponents. Such play occurs throughout the poker world and sometimes results in considerable success for the perpetrator.

The online poker world is one which features very loose (eager to call repeatedly) players. In simple terms, the longer you stay in a hand, and the more hands you are involved in, the more likely it is that you will hit some miracle cards which result in a massive pot. Decent players appreciate that the value of such play is hugely outweighed by the inevitable long-term losses you will have to endure. Frustrating though it is to be on the end of appalling play, the fact that such play exists will only serve to boost your bankroll in the long term.

The online poker room market is a competitive one, and site security and the integrity of the game are paramount for everyone. One founded rumour could destroy a multi-million dollar business.

In simple terms, the consensus within the industry and among successful players is that online poker is safe and well-regulated: the cards are generated as randomly as a computer can muster; sites will investigate – with access to every hand in question – any claims of malfeasance; top sites monitor potential collusion between players and act to prevent it, and every pot, side pot, split pot and house rake, is calculated and processed perfectly.

None of this can be said of a live game.

Finally, there are many home games, card-room games, even casino games – there's a famous one in London – where you will face collusion against you by regular players. The integrity of the shuffle and deal is not always assured, and the ability to scrutinise play at a later stage just does not exist. Simply, then, online play offers a safer (probably the safest) environment in which to play poker, than any other game in which you've participated.

Downloading the Software

Ensure that you have basic Internet security, such as a reputable, modern browser (which all carry basic anti-virus programs) or your own pre-downloaded anti-virus software. Frankly, if you are using the Internet for any reason without such basic protection, you risk any information you share being grabbed by someone else or your system being infected by a potentially catastrophic virus.

Using your own or someone else's young kids to download the software for your poker site is quite acceptable, indeed these days *de rigueur*. Once downloaded, ask them to create a shortcut from the desktop for you, so that you can click on a poker room icon and the software will start up immediately, and you will be taken to your chosen site.

Once inside, you can often take a tour of what the site looks like before downloading or you can download and then investigate. If you don't like what you see, all software will have an "uninstall" option which you can choose at any time to remove the program from your computer. Again, the computer savvy, of any age, can advise you.

Exploring the Poker Site

Some sites will make you fill in a basic application form before you can look at their site. This will allow you to use their "Play Money" at a few tables.

You will have to pick a nickname at this point and, although you can change it later, it is easier to come up with one you like now and stick with it.

Picking a Screen Name

Your anonymity online is an advantage. Therefore, I wouldn't use your own name, or utilise any option to display a photograph of yourself.

There is quite an element of role-playing in poker, and a little acting is enjoyable, so you may wish to invent a poker-playing persona for yourself and pick a name, or avatar image to fit this. As with most online activity, this can be deliberately misleading: you can change age, gender, race, religion – whatever you like.

When you see the names of other players, be aware that they have probably been chosen for your benefit. If you encounter "Dizzy-Blonde", that player may be a middle-aged male poker professional who is trying to give the impression that he's a part-time player dilly-dallying online in between reading celebrity magazines. "DarkDestroyer12" may be a retired school mistress who is only just learning the game. Similarly, "Loose-as-Hell" is probably tight and aggressive and "Mrs Rock" plays every hand and bluffs at half the pots. You never can tell but, as a general rule, poor and less experienced players (the vast majority of the players you will encounter) tend to opt to mislead: in name, demeanor, style of play and chat.

Having done this, your first stop will now be the lobby. This page will look pretty complicated at first, but you should imagine that it is a real lobby to your local card club and, within it, you can access all the information that you could possibly want about the various games that are going on, what will be coming up in the next few days and weeks, and what special offers or exciting news there might be to share.

The Lobby
There are many slight variations but what a lobby page basically looks like is shown in Fig. 1 on page 23.

The top row shows the types of poker available. Click on the style of poker you wish to play and you will see a list appear indicating all the different tables in play and what is happening at each.

We are focusing on NL Texas Hold 'Em. So click on **Hold 'Em** which, being the most popular, is usually the first box.

The second row shows the headings for each column. Working from left to right in this example, this is what each shows:

Table   In a live card room, these are often numbered; in an online poker room, they usually have names.

Stakes   This shows the small blind and big blind level. In a cash game, these stay constant throughout the game.

Type   This shows whether the Hold 'Em game is Limit Poker (Limit), Pot-Limit Poker (PL), or No-Limit Poker (NL).

Players   This shows how many players are at a table. If the computer indicates: 7/9 that means that there are seven players present out of a possible nine seats; 4/6 shows four players at a table with a maximum of six seats.

Waiting   This indicates how many people, if any, are waiting to come into the table. If there are a lot of them, perhaps they know that there is a madman there who likes giving away his chips to everyone, a veritable Vesuvius of chips, who just keeps erupting. I call this a "feeding frenzy".

Av. Pot   The figure here shows the size of the average pot.

Plrs/Flop This shows how many players are seeing the flop each hand.

Hands p/h This shows how many hands are being played per hour.

We'll look at what we can learn from all these statistics – and what we learn is vital – in Table Selection (page 34).

If you have picked a major online poker site, there will be hundreds of tables in play, 24 hours a day, at every stake from 5c/10c right up to, perhaps, $1,000/$2,000!

To play at a table, you usually double-click the name in the lobby and you are taken straight to the game. But resist the temptation to do that right now.

HOLD 'EM	OMAHA		STUD	RAZZ	SIT & GO		TOURNAMENTS
Table	Stakes	Type	Players	Waiting	Av. Pot	Plrs/Flop	Hands p/h
Trumpton	$1/$2	NL	9/9	0	$63.07	16%	81
Sphinx	$1/$2	NL	8/9	0	$59.40	42%	61
Norwich	$1/$2	NL	9/9	1	$21.87	18%	64
Atlantic	$1/$2	NL	9/9	2	$19.75	41%	69
Rumble	$1/$2	NL	0/6	0			
Thorax	$1/$2	NL	4/6	0	$15.50	50%	91

Fig. 1.   The Lobby

Play Money

It's worth having a go at a table with play money now if you have never played online before. You can use this unending supply of imaginary money (you can almost always top it up by visiting the Cashier, see page 29) to play a few hands, get used to the site, the way you place your bets, check, fold, etc.

As a way of practising poker, however, play money is a complete waste of time. Since you keep score at poker using money – the chips in front of you – if you don't play for real money, no one pays any attention to the scores, and, consequently, play money games are not poker and won't help you to improve your game any more than playing for "fun" at home with your children, pets and stuffed toys.

At the Table

Assuming that you are still reading this section because you are an online poker virgin, we'll now run through what you will encounter. Many of the details will be discussed in greater detail in the forthcoming chapters. This section is purely to give you an idea of what you will encounter.

You can watch a table (or tables) at play, observing the action and getting used to the feel of the online game, or you could enter a play money table. Whilst this won't help your poker, it will look like a real money table and so you can become acquainted with your poker room surroundings. Almost all sites offer you the chance to alter the look of the card room from the colour of the decks of cards with which you play, to the background scenery in the room. Some offer you the chance to choose an avatar – a cartoon character – to represent you; others even let you download a photograph of yourself to appear in your "seat".

When you get to your table, you may be allocated a seat, or you may have a chance to pick where you would like to sit. As we will see later, this is a very important decision but, either way, having been seated, you will be invited to buy-in for an amount which must be between the stated minimum and maximum amounts. What you should do here will also be discussed a bit later.

If you take a look at Fig. 2 (overleaf) you will see yourself in a standard online poker room (they all differ to a greater or lesser extent). This table has only six seats available at it, others offer you 9- or 10-seater tables. The table you choose will be determined by your own preference and playing style, which we'll look at later also.

Take a look at the other players at your table. Beneath their nickname you will see a figure. This represents how much money they have at the table. Later, we will see why this can be important to note.

While you are looking at the table, the game will continue. Online, the action never stops . . . And it seems to be very fast action. The dealer button (shown in Fig. 2 as a D in a circle) moves clockwise around the table as it does usually, the small blind and big blind get placed by the computer (usually) and then the cards are dealt. Each player has about 30 seconds to decide whether to fold, check, bet, call, raise or re-raise.

When it comes to your turn, you will know that it is you to play, since a graphical or numerical counter will appear under your name, or at the top of the screen, showing you how much time you have left to make your decision. If you do not act within this time, the computer folds you or, if there has not yet been any betting, checks your hand. A few sites offer you the chance to request extra time to make your decision. However, online poker is a fast-moving game – it is what makes it so hugely popular – and you will soon become accustomed to the speed.

Buttons and Boxes
Online poker rooms offer a variety of different options. These are the ones to which you should pay attention:

Chat Box
Almost all online poker rooms offer you the chance to chat with your opponents, and even let observers chip in. My very

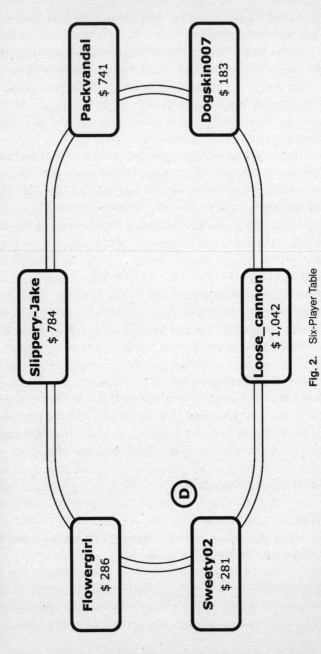

Table: Sphinx
Texas NL Hold 'Em $2/ $4

Fig. 2. Six-Player Table

strong advice to you now – and throughout this book – is to turn off the chat altogether. You will probably do this by clicking on an "Options" button or menu and checking the box which says "All Chat Off" or "No Chat Whatsoever".

Not only will this provide more space on your screen but you can concentrate on the game.

Sounds

While you are in the Options menu, take a look at the Sounds options. I don't like some mechanical dealer's voice yabbering at me, so I check "Dealer's Voice Off", but I quite like the clacking of chips when someone places a bet, and the clinking of a big pile of chips being pushed towards me. If you don't, check the "All Sounds Off" box.

Auto Post Blinds

You will have the option of checking this box and I recommend that you do. When it is your turn to place small or big blinds, the computer will do this for you. This speeds up the game and allows you to focus on the important things.

Sit Out Next Hand

Self-explanatory and not really recommended since, if you sit out when it is your turn to place the blind bets, you will be forced to place them later. However, if the doorbell rings or the dog needs letting out, this is the box you check.

Stand Up or Leave Table

Pressing this button, or checking this box, means that you are leaving the game. Once you do this, you may not get back to the same table again as your place may be taken immediately by another player waiting to buy-in.

If you leave the table having made money, should you wish to return to the same table you will usually be forced to return with the maximum buy-in, or even the amount with which you left. So, there's no strategic reason to leave your table unless you have decided that it isn't the one for you – which is a very good reason.

Re-Buy Chips
Assuming that you have sufficient funds in your account, you can re-buy chips, up to the maximum permitted at the table, at any time when you are not directly involved in a hand. Click the "Re-Buy Chips" or "Top-Up Chips" button and you will be shown a second screen showing you how much you can buy.

Action Buttons
These are the buttons that you click on to make your decisions: fold, check, call or raise.

Unless you are playing Limit Poker (when the computer indicates the raise you are permitted to make), before pressing the raise button you select the size of your bet. You can usually type this figure into a box, or scroll through a list of figures. Since No-Limit Hold 'Em is the favoured game online, that may be anything from a few cents to an all-in bet of several hundreds or thousands of dollars.

Auto-Action Boxes and Buttons
These are options such as "Check/Fold" or "Fold to Any Bet".

These should not be utilised, since they may give extra information to your opponents (see page 95).

Fold all Losing Hands
This is the one Auto-Action box that I would check. This means that, when you are in a showdown, any time that your hand does not win, the computer mucks your cards without displaying them. Since it is almost always a bad idea to show your cards, this seems a good idea. Experienced players who take the time, and make the effort, to study hand records, may be able to see which cards you were holding, but very few players take advantage of this.

Other Auto-Action buttons and boxes should be left alone. Do not use the "Call Any Bet" option, because you have no idea what might happen before then. Leave alone any other option which persuades you to make a decision before it is your turn to act. When it's your turn, you should give the impression of consideration by pausing for five to ten seconds even if you really know that you are going to fold. This gives a much stronger, more focused impression to your opponents – and goes towards standardising your betting timing, which may occlude your ambitions – and that is always good.

House Rake

You may notice that the pot total (which is usually displayed next to the pile of chips in the middle of the table) is a strange number, with small decimals at the end. This is because the way online poker sites make their money at cash games is by removing a small percentage of each pot. The figures vary slightly, and usually nothing is removed if the hand ends before the flop. Don't worry about the rake because it happens automatically on every hand, and you really only pay it when you win a pot.

Cashier

Finally, having looked at everything carefully, it's time to put your money down on the table – metaphorically. Click on the button which takes you to the site's Cashier (there's always a Cashier button somewhere – often, it's flashing!).

Now, you have to fill in proper name and address details, submit a credit card, or use an online payment method, to fund your account.

Most credit cards protect you from online fraud – check that yours does – and all the good sites are very secure. When you first transfer some money to your poker account, make it a small amount. You are still in the learning stage and you want to avoid losing too much. Once you have established yourself online, you will want to start with a good, solid, healthy bankroll.

And now, you are ready to play. From here, it is assumed that you know your way about an online poker site and that you have a decent basic, general knowledge of the game. If you don't feel confident, pick up a copy of my poker book written specifically for beginners, *Texas Hold 'Em Poker – Begin and Win*, and run through all the basics that you need to start a lifetime of happy – and successful – poker.

2

BEFORE YOU PLAY

You won't like it, but I want to stop you playing poker – at least for a few minutes. What you do before you play will prove absolutely crucial to your success or failure at the poker table. Depending on your chosen stake, we're talking hundreds, thousands, even hundreds of thousands of dollars' worth of difference.

The vast majority of online players, log on, click on the first table they encounter and start playing. I don't blame them; I like to get going too.

However, if you want to succeed, you must curb such impulses and spend a few moments on preparation. This will be counter-intuitive and may lead you to make excuses such as, "It's a game, it's meant to be fun!", "I only have a couple of hours to myself – I don't want to waste any time mucking about" and, particularly, "You're making it sound like hard work."

I promise you that this isn't hard work, and you'll enjoy your game far more if you are winning. Frankly, if you can't display the patience and dedication to carry out these simple preparatory tasks (and it took me way too long, and lost me far too much money to figure out their importance) then you don't deserve to win.

Mood

If you're in a bad mood, negative frame of mind, paranoid and depressed, or a steaming bad temper, don't play poker. I can't emphasize this enough. Virtually every session where I could have won money, but instead lost, coincided with me being in one of the above frames of mind.

To succeed at poker – as at most things I guess – you need to feel confident, positive, and relaxed. Because poker can be such an emotional game you want, at the outset at least, to be in the best possible state. The moment you feel yourself becoming emotional, taking personally the out-rageous fortunes of luck, or becoming vindictive and aggres-sive towards your opponents, I urge you: stop playing for at least a few minutes. Better yet, give it up for the day. Failing to do so has cost me hundreds of pots and thousands of dollars.

Now, think a moment. If you can walk away in these situations and most others cannot, when you are playing in the best possible mental state you will be ready to take on these undisciplined souls and part them from their money.

As well as an instinctive desire to win, to be seen to win and enjoy it, poker is very much a game about discipline, patience, and self-knowledge. Combine these elements, develop them within yourself, and you will be on the way to eliminating loss-making situations before a single card has been dealt.

Bankroll

Your aim is to grow your bankroll, slowly and reasonably consistently. As your skill increases, the size of game in which you wish to play may increase, but your poker successes must pay for that promotion to the higher leagues. If they don't, you're not ready for them yet.

If you worry about money, what you have left with which to play, then you cannot concentrate on your game. This can be very detrimental to your success.

Because poker is a game where there can be long streaks of

success and failure, it is vital to have a sizeable enough bankroll to cope with the failures.

My recommendation is to have TWENTY times your usual buy-in available in your bankroll.

That means that if you are planning on depositing $500 in your account, then you should be buying into each game, or playing tournaments, with just $25. If you think you are a mid-range player, and you plan to buy-in to tables for $400, then you are going to need $8,000 in your bankroll. Yup! You read that right: $8,000. You may have been playing with a quarter of this collateral, or even less, and that could be a major contributing factor to your lack of success.

However good you are at poker, you will have losing sessions and you will have several in a row. This is statistically inevitable. The key is that if you lose ten sessions and you know that you still have half your bankroll remaining, the losses fall into proportion and you will not allow the size of your bankroll to determine playing decisions. At poker, you cannot be afraid of money, or let its sudden appearance or disappearance influence your play. Much of that influence may be sub-conscious – which is all well and good – until it starts disrupting your play: then, it is a real problem.

There is no shame playing lower-stake games. I have friends who play very modest games online, enjoy every minute of them, and come out winners every year. Sometimes you will find you can win easily at one level, and lose consistently at the next level up. Just drop back down to where you are happy and keep winning.

When I first started playing higher-stake games, I found that I was still winning, but not nearly as much as I used to win in the lower-stake game. Also, although I felt that I was witnessing superior poker and learning from that, I found the experience quite stressful and draining. At the end of a few months, I found I was winning more money, and having much more fun in my old mid-range games. As you play, you'll find the game that suits you – stick to it – and only move up slowly.

g this advice means that you must move down in
ur game then, unless you are a consistent winner
ent games, please do it. You will find that it forms
werful winning formula.

Table Selection (Cash Games)

I know that you don't want to waste time staring at the lobby
before playing but, again, some order and discipline here
will earn you money. Imagine that you are standing on the
first tee of a golf course which was new to you. Surely,
before teeing off, you would ask about bunker positions, the
best line into the green, or look at a course planner? So it
should be with poker. The information in the lobby can be
used to help you to choose a table where you are far more
likely to win. Not to spend a few moments each time you
log in for a session checking this out would be to throw
money away.

Interpretation of Lobby Information

Let's take a look back at Fig. 1, on page 23, at the list of tables
in play for NL Hold 'Em in your chosen stake range and see
what can be learnt from the statistics on offer:

The key columns are the *Average Pot Size (Av. Pot)* and the
Percentage of Players seeing Flop (Plrs/Flop). Together,
these reveal the nature and make-up of each game (assuming
that there hasn't been a major change of players at the table in
the last few minutes).

This is the basic, but crucial, read on the games you will
encounter:

1. Large pot size, combined with low percentage of players
   seeing the flop =
   tight/aggressive game with pre-flop raising and re-raising.

2. Large pot size, combined with high percentage of players
   seeing the flop =

loose/aggressive game – many players in pot, calling the blinds and calling raises.

3. Small pot size, combined with low percentage of players seeing the flop =
   tight/passive game – only pre-flop calling, or a raise and one caller.

4. Small pot size, combined with high percentage of players seeing the flop =
   loose/passive game – players calling pre-flop, but folding post-flop.

In these descriptions, "tight" and "loose" refer to the keenness to call bets: the former being reluctant and choosey when it comes to calling, the latter being keen to put their money into the pot whatever the odds might suggest.

"Passive" and "aggressive" refer to playing styles. The former suggests a tendency to check and call; the latter to bet, raise and re-raise.

The game you will choose will depend on the basic style that you enjoy playing, bearing in mind that, fundamentally, playing a style opposite to the prevailing one at your table will often prove successful.

For online cash games, I like to play a tight/aggressive style – that is to say, I pass a lot of hands, wait for a good starting hand and good position against an opponent(s) on whom I have some information and, when I get a decent hand, play it strongly by betting, raising and re-raising. For me, then, "Norwich" and, particularly "Atlantic", look good and likely to lead to profit, and they are the ones I will seek out.

"Norwich" features a low pot size and small number of players per flop, which suggests a tightness and predictability about the players, and that there is little raising. I think that I will cause a bit of trouble there.

"Atlantic" has a high number of players seeing each flop, but a low pot size, so there can't be much raising, and everyone is a bit loose. Again, that sounds attractive to me, because I intend to raise and single out my opponents for rough treatment.

"Sphinx" looks dangerous because, since there is a high percentage of players seeing the flop and the pot size is high, then it seems like several players are calling every raise. If there are multiple calls of your initial raise, the value of your hand falls. For example, if you raise with AA and get only one caller, you are at least 80 per cent on to win the hand. If, with the same AA, you get four callers, you become odds against to take the pot, and your opportunity to price out draws (by betting so much that the odds become negative for callers) post-flop becomes much more expensive because of the size of the pot and the resulting pot odds for anyone drawing.

Incidentally, this is why experts have such a tough time in loose, low standard games which might, at first, seem rich pickings.

The expert waits for his decent hand and position and raises; five players call him. Now, it is extremely likely that one of them will hit something pretty good on the flop, and the expert's good hand is in big danger. I've been caught, time and time again, in this situation in low-stake online games and friendly home games. It's very frustrating unless you hit some big flops, and this is why good players tend to avoid these weak, loose games.

"Trumpton" looks pretty expert or, at the very least, fearless, and whilst it could offer potentially big profits, the swings are likely to be huge and indigestion-forming. There are only a couple of players seeing each flop but the pot size is very big. This looks like raising and re-raising and a lot of betting. Why volunteer for such treatment when there are hundreds of tables from which to choose?

Stack Sizes

On some sites you are able to preview exactly who the players are at any given table and their stack sizes; on others, you will have to join the table before seeing the personnel and stack-size information.

Either way, this can be valuable knowledge, since there are messages there:

• A table with all low stacks might suggest that they are losing players, perhaps recently mauled by a good player, but it does not mean that playing there will be easy. Frustrated, outplayed, players may feel like big pre-flop raises, or all-in moves. This table can be profitable but there are two negatives: they don't have much money to lose to you and you may be forced to gamble more than you would wish.

• A table with one very big stack and several low ones suggests that the expert player is still there. If you feel that the game still looks ripe, ensure you sit with big stack to your right, allowing him to act before you are forced into a big decision.

• A table with stacks all averaging, roughly, a little less than combined maximum buy-ins is likely to be a new table or a tough, tight game, with no apparent weak links.

All these elements add to your knowledge of a table before you enter it.

Hands Played Per Hour

A table playing a very high number of hands per hour may be ripe for someone to come in and slow them down, frustrating their urge for constant action and adrenalin rushes.

A table with a particularly low hand rate may cause your blood pressure to rise and your focus to be distracted. Something in the region of 50-80 hands per hour for 6-player tables, and 40-60 for 9/10-player tables sounds roughly like average online timings.

Six-Player Tables and Nine-/Ten-Player Tables

The strategy for success varies substantially between these two games. Do not think that they are the same.

Because a short-handed table means that the blinds will come around to you far more frequently than a full 9/10-player table, a 6-player table (often with a player sitting out or a space available) requires a proactive strategy with a far wider range of calling, raising and re-raising hands. You need good post-flop playing skills, and to be prepared to play hands with a lower total value. To play very tight at one of these tables is to watch your blinds come around very fast and whittle away your stack.

Many more experienced players enjoy six-handed games since there is much more action than at tables with nine or ten players, and post-flop skills are one of the attributes which distinguish top players from the masses. However, choose to play at a 6-player table because it suits your own game, because you win playing short-handed games, and not because you find the action at a larger table too slow. Patience, as will be oft repeated, is essential to success.

A 9/10-player table allows you time to assess your opposition, pick your spots to take action, and to wait for some decent hands before entering the action. For less experienced players, this is certainly the best option and, as a result, the more experienced player is likely to find some rich pickings at the 9/10-player tables, whereas the short-handed games are more often populated by players of a higher standard.

Once again, the ideal here is to find a 9/10-seater table with one or two loose players whom you can pick off individually. A big table with multiple loose callers represents more dangerous waters.

Where to Sit

Where you sit at a table is hugely important, and substantially affects your ability to win money. To sit at a table which you have identified as good for you, but in the wrong seat, will be worse than to sit in the right seat at a less suitable table. This is why you often see so many players waiting to play at a particular table: they are waiting not only to play in that game with those players, but to play in a specific spot (or spots).

In simple terms, you want to sit:

• With the tight, aggressive, betting and raising player(s) on your right.

• With the loose, calling, checking player(s) on your left.

This is because to have raisers and bettors on your left means that it is tough to see a flop cheaply, as they will often up-the-ante pre-flop.

To have those players acting before you (on your right) means that you can see what they're up to before you have to act, allowing you to re-raise or fold pre-flop.

It is a big advantage if the players who come after you usually just call or check. You can often slip into a hand cheaply, and even receive free cards post-flop. If they actually manage a raise, you know you are up against a big hand and can act accordingly.

Having these styles of players placed correctly around you reduces the amount of stress you are likely to encounter and improves your reading of your opponents' cards.

If you can't sit where you want to at a table, give strong consideration to selecting another table or placing yourself on the waiting list and seeing which seats become available in the next few minutes.

Buying-In

Have a big wad! Buy into each table with the maximum permitted.

To buy into a game with half the maximum, or an odd figure of your remaining bankroll, is to display weakness and uncertainty from the outset. It will be seized upon by good players, and the feeling of being constantly behind everyone else will be re-enforced.

Not only should you buy into each game with the maximum available (or, in relation to the blinds, a very solid sum) to demonstrate that you are a serious, solid player, but you should also have a substantial bankroll for when a series of bad beats (which everyone, even the very best, experiences pretty regularly) leaves you winded.

The recommendation here is only to invest 5 per cent of your initial bankroll for the buy-in at each table. So, if you are buying-in for $200, you should have started with $4,000 in your account. If a horrible run of losing sessions costs you only 20-30 per cent of your bankroll, then you can keep the lousy session(s) from dominating your thoughts, and concentrate on steadily regaining ground.

Also, with a solid bankroll, when you are having a rough ride, you are more likely to desist from playing on blindly, possibly on tilt, and instead take the much-needed short break. At the very least, switch tables, knowing you have a sufficient bankroll to get you back in business again once you've calmed down.

Taking Notes
Knowing your opponents, and occluding your own identity and playing styles, is a big plus factor for you as a poker player. I have dozens of notebooks filled with comments and observations about the players I have encountered online. However, in recent years, all the major sites have added a note-taking facility to their software, whereby you can click (usually a double click or a right click) on a specific player at your table and make notes on their play, or read what you have written already.

Whilst there are huge advantages to this addition, there are some down sides too: your notes do not carry over from one site to another; a player changing names can foil your careful analysis of his/her play.

However, since most online players use a favourite site most of the time, calling into others on occasion, there is still real value to be had from using the built-in note-taking software.

For connected reasons, to change your own screen name and identity on a regular basis is a fine idea. You do not want your opponents to have as accurate, up-to-date notes on you as you do on them. To reassure you, however, the number of players who bother to take notes is pretty small (despite the advantages of doing so being pretty big).

Whilst it is easy and sometimes satisfying to note that a particular opponent is "idiotic and incredibly lucky", this is unlikely to help you in the future. You want to make specific comments on their play, their choice of cards to call and raise, and an estimate of their playing style. I also like to put a date for each of my entries (just a month and year) so that I don't look at a note from two years ago and then wonder why this particular player seems to have improved beyond recognition.

Everyone has their own style, but this might be what a note on a player looks like:

02/07   Seems patient, waiting for spots, aggressive, re-raised button raise in bb with AJs, but never called one of my raises.

11/07   Still tight/aggressive, seems good and strong. Only raised X2 with AA in 1st pos in 6-player game, usually raises X3 or X4 pre-flop.

I am getting the picture that this player is reliable, doesn't call raises lightly, and is to be shown respect. However, he just raised twice the big blind with AA under the gun, so perhaps that is a little tell when he has a huge hand in early position (it often is).

I am still only building up a picture of this guy, but when he raises or calls a raise, he seems to have a hand, so I can place him on a variety of good hands in these situations and probably eliminate speculative calls.

I would like three or four entries to be sure of my basic read of this guy, but even this information is going to help me enormously when it comes to making big decisions.

When you have played on a site for a few months, you will find that, when you join a new table, several of the players are known to you, with their notes readily available. You may choose to leave the table again, or you may find that you have just the personnel you are looking for. The more work you do building up your notes, the easier the game will become in terms of assessing what opponents have when they take various actions. To have information on opponents from the outset of a game is a huge, money-making advantage to you – and the first time you win a big pot, or make a great lay-down because of it, it will unquestionably be worth the effort you put in.

Poker Buddies
Many sites offer a facility to make a particular player one of your "Buddies" or "Poker Friends". You click on them and add them to your list of buddies. Then, when you sign on, you can see which of them is online with you and, supposedly, meet up for a game at a particular table or just chew the fat together in a chatbox. This is all very charming and delightful, and a total and complete distraction from your business. Yes, use the Poker Buddies button to mark certain players – the ones you want to play against! The loose ones, the ones who are passive and lacking knowledge, the ones whose play you have registered and can counter effectively, the ones whom you beat consistently. Each time you come online, check for your "buddies" and make a beeline for their tables.

Hand Records
By requesting these from your site – you can usually access them at the click of a button – you can review every hand

played at your table, together with all cards that legally would be shown to you (online, losing cards are often mucked, even though in a live game, you would be permitted to see them). In this way, you can watch how a big pot came together, how you outplayed, or were outplayed by, a particular opponent, and note the styles involved.

You can watch how a particularly successful player at your table gained momentum and dominated your game. You can even print out the actions you took and discuss the hand with a friend or more experienced player. The hand records offer you an amazing resource for learning and improving your game. Do not ignore them.

Some of the best sites online have hand records which are difficult to read and interpret because they are poorly laid out. The quality of the hand records and their layout and ease of interpretation may be a factor as to which site(s) you choose – they can be that important.

Stats

All top sites will offer a button called "Stats". By clicking this button, you will receive up-to-the-minute statistics on your play so far this session. Some sites provide individual table statistics, others combine all statistics for the tables you have played at in that session. You will have the option to re-set the stats and start again at any time.

The stats available on different sites all vary slightly. Let's take a look at what you might see and what these figures tell you:

Percentage of Flops Seen

This includes big blinds where there is no pre-flop raise. A high percentage of flops seen suggests a looseness to your play; a lower percentage, tightness.

What are the correct percentages? In poker, there is rarely a correct answer – at least not every time – and much will depend on your favoured style. As a very rough guide, for short-handed games (6-player tables) around 33 per cent would suggest a moderately aggressive game; for full tables (with nine or ten players) around 15-20 per cent would represent a similar level of assertiveness. This is not to say that you can't double or halve those figures – they are only the roughest of guidelines.

Percentage of Call/Check, Bet, Raise
A successful strategy is usually an aggressive one, so you would not want to see your call and check stats at too high a figure. You want to see bets and raises as a good proportion of your action. Re-raising is generally a rare bird, but you would probably see a small percentage here in a rounded game. However, you might be playing at a table where there is a guy raising every hand, and you are letting him make all the action and trapping him happily from time to time, calling down his endless betting.

Hands Won Without Showdown
You want to win as many hands as possible without showing down your hand and, if you are playing aggressive poker, this is what will happen. You should be able to note a correlation between a higher percentage of betting and raising and more hands won without a showdown.

Hands Won at Showdown
If you're hitting great cards or playing at a table of calling stations, you might have a high percentage here but, normally, you would want this figure to be much less than the one above, since you should be blowing your opponents out of the hand (for all sorts of reasons) before you have to show your cards.

The stats from just one session will only give you a glimpse of your style but, as you note the stats over a period of time, you will discover whether, basically, you are an aggressive or passive player; loose or tight. To know this, to see it spelt out in front of you, will help you towards the self-knowledge and understanding required to succeed at poker.

Session Notes
Take a notebook and make a quick entry for every table at which you play: date, time of day, how you feel, the game you played in, stake, buy-in and cash out, number of players, whether you picked the table carefully. Jot down your results, and your stats.

There will come a time when you feel so moved to study these notes and extrapolate your conclusions. You will almost certainly find that they support this new regimen you are attempting. More importantly, you may discover that when you are in a confident mood and you play aggressively, you win much more than when you are tired and playing passively. Or vice versa. Whatever you discover after quite a few months will help you to shape your play to the style that wins the most and brings you maximum pleasure.

You will want to dispense with these activities and get on with the game. I urge you to fight those impulses. If you want to win money and enjoy yourself, you have to earn it. Every successful poker player has gone through similar – and usually far, far more rigorous processes – to become the success he is today. This is easy stuff – but it is unquestionably worth doing.

3

CASH GAME STRATEGY

You buy-in to a game you have selected, looking at the criteria discussed in the previous chapter. Hopefully, you have:

• Notes on some of the players.

• You are in the seat you have selected as being positive for you.

• You have the maximum buy-in chips in front of you.

In the early stages of buying-in, it is vital to observe the game carefully the whole time. You are looking for information, clues and, perhaps, the weak link. The age-old poker proverb, "If you can't spot the sucker at your table within ten minutes – it's you", is reasonably profound.

You should already suspect suckers at your table, because you have selected it carefully, but now, you must hunt them down. This does not require you to get involved in any big hands and, during the first ten or fifteen minutes at the table, I advise against it. This is simply because you have not yet had time to assess your opponents, and that leaves you short of all the information you would like to have before making a big decision.

During this early phase, stick to sure things; don't commit too many chips. To lose half your stack on a gamble in the first fifteen minutes is very common online. The desire to play over-rules the sensible preparations required. When you start to keep session notes, you may well notice this tendency to lose pots early on; if you can eliminate those losses, both your psychological well-being and your bankroll will be in better shape.

Standard Strategy

My favoured standard strategy for cash games, based on my preferred game: 9/10-player mid-range stake (say $1/$2 to $2/$5, maybe $5/$10), would be to play a tight/aggressive game. That is to say, be tight in the way you pick the hands you play, and then be aggressive in the way you play them: raising, raising.

This sounds exciting but, regretfully, I confess that it is usually not. To make money at poker consistently, you have to know the game, but you must also possess great self-control. When the deck is cold and, on the few hands you play, the cards run bad, it's easy to tell yourself that this is supposed to be fun, that it's just a game, and compromise all your carefully planned strategy for a few quick thrills. But, I guarantee you, that is just what the good players are waiting for – and they will be ruthless in cleaning up. It's clear that you want to be among these experts, and that is why you must develop a strong, calm level of patience. This is never shown on television: the hours of folding, calling for a cheap flop, and folding some more – but it is the fate of good cash game players the world over; the fate of the successful ones.

Positions and Starting Hands

Let's take a look at some starting hands and, in doing so, describe the positions at the table:

Early position   The first third of players to act after the big blind.

Mid position   The second third of players to act.

Late position   The last third of players to act.

To bet in early position risks a later raise, and/or re-raise, which results in you folding and wasting your initial bet. Your hands will generally be stronger the earlier you call or raise.

To bet in mid position is safer, with fewer players to act after you.

To bet in late position is relatively safe since there will only be one or two players to act, plus the small and big blinds, who will have to act first on all subsequent rounds of betting and who are, for that reason, in a disadvantageous position.

AA, KK, AK, QQ – these hands need raising in any position. Raising in early position may buy you only the blinds, but, equally, you have selected a table with callers, so hopefully, you have one.

Merely to call on these hands is usually wrong online. The tendency to call is always increased online – it's so easy to click that button – and then you may have a five- or six-person flop. That spells bad news for your hand.

Re-raise with these hands. Make it good and big and then you will find out where you stand. If a solid player calls you, you know you are up against another big hand. That you routinely do this with all four of these hands will hide what you have – they are four very different starting hands.

JJ, 1010, 99, 88 and AQ, AJs (the small "s" here, and throughout, stands for suited – of the same suit) – these can be danger hands anyway. A call in early and mid positions, and a raise in later position, will suffice, although more aggressive play would see 1010, 99, and 88 being played strongly with a raise or even, re-raise in any position.

Low pairs, ace-low suited, suited connectors – these hands are reasonably safe because, unless you hit the flop, you can lay them down easily post-flop. With these hands, you are aiming for trips, a nut flush (or cheap draw) or straight-flush draws on the suited connectors. They are worth a cheap call in mid and late positions.

All other cards get mucked: all those K9 and Q10 cards. Those hands hit rarely, but usually they just cost and cost and cost.

How Much to Raise?

Because the vast majority of online players are loose, there will be a tendency for players to call more raises. For this reason, I favour a standard raise of four and a half times the big blind. This seems big enough to dissuade most of the cheeky chasers, but affordable for players trying to hit great flops (with hands like mid-pairs and promising suited-connectors – both of which offer poor odds of hitting).

You might decide always to raise four and a half times the big blind and, indeed, playing every decent hand the same way is not a terrible strategy. Usually, however, I would favour varying the raise – making it X4 sometimes, X5 other times. Just ensure that you don't decide on your raise based on your hand. You should tell yourself that whatever raise you make is completely unconnected to your two cards.

Following up Your Raise

If you raise and then check, you are displaying weakness – almost all of the time. You could have flopped the nuts and want to induce some bets into you. But, generally, the best way to play, whether you've hit the flop, or whether it's missed you completely, is to follow up your pre-flop raise with a decent bet now.

You may take a player off what is now the best hand. You may force one or more lay-downs from similarly missed flops. You may well persuade a marginal drawing hand to fold . . . Lots of ways to win. And, if your opponent calls or raises, you now have information and you can decide whether to make a move, or lay down your hand quietly. Of course, of those times your opponent calls or raises and you are marked as the losing hand, you may actually have a very strong hand, and can move your chips in, slowly or fast (I recommend fast).

Raising Follow-Up Bets

Because most decent players are aware that to follow up a raise pre-flop with a bet on the flop is sound standard strategy, you should prepare a counter. Probably less than one time in four will the initial pre-flop raiser believe that he's flopped the best hand. Even if he is pretty sure, a re-raise will either smoke him out, or plant a seed of doubt in his mind.

Obviously a re-raise will take out your opponent (and, rarely, opponents) when he has missed the flop with AK or AQ, but it may also persuade KK to lay down to a simple ace on the board, or frighten QQ with either an ace or king. So, a re-raise looks a possible play as a total bluff, and a really good option for a drawing bluff.

When the board pairs low or middle cards, this bluff re-raise can, not only force a laydown, but also play on the mind of your opponent. If the flop comes J88 and you raise his follow-up bet, he may even lay down a high pocket pair, and wonder what card you held to go with your 8. If you had your chat-box open – which you don't – you'd probably see some unimaginative verbal abuse.

Raise a slightly larger amount than your opponent's bet; there is no need to bet more – the re-raise action itself will certainly provoke a reaction worth watching.

Having raised the post-flop bet, assuming that your opponent chooses not to fold, you see the turn, and then may get to see a cheap, or cheaper, river. This has given you maximum opportunities to win the hand and ensures that when you hit and go all-in, your opponent will think twice before following up his raise the next time he misses the flop. In fact, he may be more reluctant to raise in the first place.

So, this play bolsters your image as aggressive, begins to play on the mind of your opponents, and it offers you the chance to steal a few hands which otherwise you might have laid down yourself.

Use sparingly and only once you have judged your opponent capable of a good laydown; if your opponent calls everything down, this won't work.

Re-Raising

You won't, generally, win by calling. More than this, to re-raise demonstrates a positive, aggressive attitude – adding again to your ideal poker persona. To re-raise is to sow a seed of doubt that, even if your opponent hits his hand, he may not win the pot. In the short term, against medium-strength opponents, you will make them question their own judgments of their hands and force lay-downs, whether or not you are ahead at the time. In the long term, you will inhibit opponents from betting or raising, because they fear that you will take aggressive action against them. To re-raise strongly limits opportunities for your opponents to stay in the hand – at the correct odds – and try to hit their drawing hands – on the turn and river. All of this moves the game the way you want it to go.

Against very strong opposition, you'd better have your bet and, against weak opponents, most of the significance is lost, the weak player tends to call you down. However, the mid-range player, and all those who think they fall into that category, know just enough to be wary of such a play. In this level of game, re-raise is not used that often (unless it is an all-in move) and therefore it carries more weight. Indeed, the right size of re-raise is usually between the size of your opponent's raise and the size of the pot.

A prime spot for a re-raise is after an early raise, or bet, which is called by more than one other player. The act of re-raising late often causes the initial raiser or bettor to fold, fearing that there are still several players to act after him. The later players may have called because they hold marginal hands or low or medium pairs and the pot seems worth the entry price. Your re-raise clearly heralds a high pair and will often persuade them to fold.

What sort of hand should you hold for such a play? Very strong to nothing much, depending on your position and whether this is your chosen moment, or spot.

Incidentally, when an opponent re-raises you, don't resent him for it. The act of re-raising has two positive effects: it warns you of possible danger; it is likely to cut out further drawing from other players, allowing you to come down head-to-head with your opponent should you choose to continue in the hand.

Trips

Flopping them is a joy but, although they look great, they are very vulnerable to drawing hands where straights and flushes can subsequently appear. For this reason, it is worth making your default play always to raise and raise big with this hand. Some online experts advocate going all-in when you hit trips because, they say, weak players often call with top pair or two pair because the all-in bet smells like a semi-bluff move. This probably works in low-stake games but, I think, at medium and high levels, you don't mind teasing one more bet out of one more player if you think you can identify his draw on the board.

When having to act first, the danger is that you check, hoping to check-raise an opponent who bets subsequently, and then no bet comes. Now, opponents have got to see the turn for free and one may have hit his draw or gained more outs. So, don't slow play trips at all.

Check-Raises

These feel hugely satisfying because you're telling the world you've tricked your opponent and you are "The Man", but sometimes they misfire catastrophically, when the size of the pot following a check-raise keeps a player on a draw he might otherwise have ditched. Often, a simple bet from you initially will maximise your up-side and minimise your potential losses.

Because a check-raise is such a show of strength it is certainly worth trying as a bluff from time to time. Many weaker players consider that a hand is over if they face a check-raise, and they fold weakly. At the very least, you have the seed of doubt planted in your opponent's mind and now a check by you on the turn may be checked to the river and you might hit a hand yet. So semi-bluffing check-raises – on the draw – and outright bluff check-raises may have some place in your arsenal when the time, the player, your position, your chip-stack, all feel right. That is the art of what poker players call "Picking your Spot". A long-awaited moment when all the factors available to you are pointing you in a gut/logical way to make a play. You aren't just waiting for cards, you are creating opportunities for yourself when the time is right.

Slow Playing
To slow play a hand and gather armfuls of chips is a thrilling experience, one in which your nerve must hold and your opponent must read you wrong. However, it is a losing strategy in the long run because there are too many possible draws out there to ensure you win sufficient big pots to cover sucking out on quite a few.

The problem with slow playing is two-fold: getting away from the hand. We're never quite sure that our good hand isn't still the best and so we tend to chase it down.

Also, cards may appear which either hit the opponent and make his hand, or serve to frighten him into not continuing in the hand if it will cost him a cent more. Therefore, an early bet, rather than the slow play, saves you from danger and maximises your chances of your opponent gambling now, when he may not be certain that you are as strong as you are.

The easiest way to deal with the lure of the slow play is to ensure you do not come into temptation. Don't slow play. When you've got the best hand, just bet it, even if it is the nuts. If he doesn't call now, it's unlikely that he'll call with an inferior hand later on. To slow play should not be part of your standard strategy for cash games, unless, on rare occasions, you are facing only one opponent on whom you believe you have some good information.

Defend Your Blinds?
I'm guessing that we all get fed up with the button raising up the pot before we, in the blinds, get to see a cheap flop with our reasonable hands. So, perhaps, we think it's worth defending the blinds (by raising) and try to put the players to our right off late-position raises?

It isn't.

The reasons are as follows: online, players at a table change regularly; you may impress one fellow on your right and then he might leave and you have to do it all over again. While you do it again, you again play in the worst possible position at the table: under the gun. If your raise is called, you will have to act first every time and the button raiser has you just where he wants you. Simply, that's not a nice spot to be in.

How often will button raisers call your re-raise? It will depend on the table. Have you picked well? Do you know the opponent to your right? Maybe you try this once and the button raiser folds. Good, try it again later by all means. Maybe, at this table, against this opponent, it's working. But, remember, online everyone calls more. So, more than likely, you'll be called, and now the defence of your hand – in the worst possible position – is costing you, not only chips, but stress.

So, no small blind protective raises. Keep all bets there ultra-strong. Rarely, you might try big blind protection, but go easy, online it's not really a worthwhile play.

(If you're playing a live home game and you know that everyone is staying around, in the same seats, for the next six hours, that's quite a different matter. Now, early table image may well pay dividends.)

Aggressive Into Draws

The temptation to call into draws, seemingly cheaply, must generally be resisted. If you miss your draw, you will have to pay again after the turn when your opponent bets again, in all likelihood with worse odds of hitting your hand. When you do hit, it should be reasonably easy for your opponent to work it out, so you will probably be paid poorly.

To raise into a draw is a solid, standard strategy, semi-bluff. You may take down the pot on the flop, or on the turn, without having a showdown. You may take it down on the river when you bet again – either with or without having made your hand. Because you are betting into the draw you are gaining chances to win the pot early and build a sizeable pot big enough to reward your endeavours. As if all this were not enough, when you do hit your hand, it may be far harder to read for an opponent, making him more likely to call your final bet or raise.

This attitude of raising into draws re-enforces the image of you as aggressive and positive, which is exactly the persona you desire. When, on rare occasions, you back down, you add the element that not all your raises are made hands, and now your opponents may take you on at just the wrong time. You're building your reputation for being tight and aggressive and your chosen opponents won't like it. Some may leave the table; others will attempt to take you on with marginal hands – and that is just what you want.

So, the next time you hold A♠ J♠ and the flop comes:

Q♠ 9♥ 4♠

This is the time to bet, or raise into this pot. You have a 35 per cent chance of hitting the nut flush, plus your ace might pair and take the hand. Take control and, when your opponent bets, do not call – raise.

Odds

You need to know the basic odds for major draws and the improvement of certain hands. After that, you should have some idea how to calculate odds quickly. The simplest route is often the best. You hold four clubs to a flush, there's one more card to come – what are the odds of hitting it? You should know the odds for this draw but, if you don't, you can work it out easily:

You can see six cards: your two, flop and turn – that leaves 46 cards unknown. Nine of those help you (the nine clubs remaining) so the odds are 9/46 or about 20 per cent.

You can also make a simple – and only rough – calculation by multiplying the number of "outs" (the cards that can help you):

- By 4 – if there are two cards to come.
- By 2 – if there is only one card to come.

That's easy enough, and accurate enough, to help you to make odds-based decisions. However, as you improve as a player the odds become less important because you will feel what is going on, your read of your opponents' cards will improve and you will be aware, almost subconsciously, of whether a play falls outside sensible odds-based parameters.

When calculating the likely pot size if you win the hand, you have to look at, not only what is already in the pot, but what might reasonably be expected to be in the pot at the end of the hand. These so-called "Implied Odds" add another temptation to go for the draw. Clearly, there is a difference between going for a draw where, if you hit your card, you might make more money, and one where it is blindingly obvious you've hit your draw and, therefore, won't get paid a cent more. For this reason, as you become more experienced, you will know when to adapt your calculation from actual "Pot Odds" – what's in the pot to win compared to what I have to pay to stay in the hand – to "Implied or Potential Odds" –

the implication being a bigger pot, one way or another.

Incidentally, there are many "Odds Calculators" online, most of them free. You tell the software your situation and it calculates exact odds immediately. It is often amazing to see confirmed that any two cards against one opponent are no worse than about 20 per cent on to win against any given hand; it is, at least, reassuring when you see your pocket aces clipped by some madman with Q7 unsuited or "off" as it is commonly described.

Table Personnel

You have selected your table with care, presumably because the style of the game suits you, and there are players present who you believe will play into your hands. Be aware of when those players leave. When they do, you are no longer playing at a carefully selected table – you are at a new table. Failing to recognise the change of personnel at a table can prove costly when you misjudge a decision, based on thinking about the player who was in that seat, instead of the one there.

The game changes: stand up, stretch your legs, preview a few tables and pick your next table.

Bluffing

There's a lot of it about online, especially in the low- and medium-stake games. You can often read these bluffs quite well, and sometimes it's a way to pick up extra donations to a pot.

To check on the river with best hand seems more successful online than in a live game, because online players like to bluff the pot at the end. Not all of them, obviously, but a decently high proportion. They've been taught that if they don't bet now, they can't win the pot (even though they shouldn't have been in the pot in the first place). So, they bet, you call, and add a little to the pot. If you're playing at a really weak table, you can "bluff" with an all-in re-raise and the best hand – and wait to get called more often than you would think possible.

Value bets – a small bet on the river you hope your

opponent may call with a losing hand – seem just fine at Limit Poker, but often don't work online playing No-Limit, at least not in low- and medium-value games.

Your own bluffing is a matter of choice and judgment, partially based on what you know about given opponents (your notes and current observations), and partly on the situation in which you find yourself at any given time. However, your aim is not to show bluff hands and retain the image that you always have what you say you have.

When playing in very weak games or low-stake games, bluffing becomes a poorer option. Indeed, the worse the player, the less likely it is that a bluff will work. Too many lousy players just want to see what you have.

Conclusion

When you start to play, and win, you will encounter many changes in your temperament. You may be confident and breezy one day and miserable and paranoid the next. Your ability to counter these swings and enjoy your games will be the biggest hurdle between you and long-term success. In the final section of tips are featured some ideas to help you.

In terms of playing style, you will have your own. If you find yourself floundering, return to the standard strategy. Here it is, in brief – and open to many variables depending on your game, the style of opponents, your bankroll, your position, your knowledge of opponents, and whether you find yourself a spot from which to act.

Our standard strategy at online cash games is to:

• Be patient, picking only good starting hands, and play those cards aggressively, betting and raising, rather than just checking and calling.

• Follow raises with bets; consider re-raising follow-up bets from others.

- Be patient.

- Avoid slow playing: bet out best hands.

- Avoid gut-shot and long-shot draws.

- Bet or raise into open-ended straight and top flush draws.

- Avoid check-raising; consider bluffing with this move.

- Be patient.

- Use re-raise to bully your opponents and make them question the value of their hands.

- Generally, be wary of defending blinds: too costly, usually not worth the risks.

- Be patient.

4

SIT & GO TOURNAMENTS

Sit & Go tournaments have been described by many as the best practice tool there is for poker, particularly tournament poker. It's cheap (or as expensive as you wish), you play a lot of poker in a set time, and you get to play in a final table scenario which, for most of us, is a rare occasion . . . especially since, these days, in a big event, there can be a field of several thousands to get through to the elusive, big-money, final table.

Some wily online poker players have found that Sit & Go tournaments provide a regular income and they play tournament poker exclusively. As you will see, many of the tips utilised in the cash game section can be utilised for tournament play also, although the more patient aspects of cash game strategy are not suitable for the pressure-cooker action of a big tournament.

Let's take a look at what it takes to win a Sit & Go.

A Sit & Go tournament operates likes a miniature live poker tournament. You start with the same number of chips as every other player at your table – usually 1,000 or 1,500 chips – and when you lose them, you're out, eliminated. The blinds start low and then rise quickly, ensuring that players must be aggressive to avoid being blinded away, and for the event to be completed within a certain time-scale – usually 60 to 90 minutes. The winner usually receives 50 per cent of the combined entry-fees, second place maybe 30 per cent, and third place 20 per cent. If there are only two winners, the division is usually 75 per cent/25 per cent.

In the lobby, click on "Sit & Go Tournaments" and you will be shown all the available games.

Unlike the cash game tables, there will be no information or stats on the game. Instead, you will see the different entry fee levels (usually from $5, through $10, $20, $30, $50, $100, $200, up to thousands of dollars) and how many players are required to form the tournament. The moment that number of players has entered, the tournament begins.

You may have a Heads-Up tournament (just two players, winner takes all); a small table (five or six players playing for first and second places); or a large table (nine or ten players, with prizes for the top three finishers).

On some sites, you can find larger Sit & Go tournaments, where there are multiple tables, and the action does not begin until twenty, forty, or however many players are indicated, are signed up.

Once you have found the game you want, say a $20 Sit & Go event, you click or double click on that game and confirm that you are paying $20 from your account to enter. On top of that, there will be an entry fee – usually between 5 per cent and 10 per cent. Once the correct number of players has entered, a new window automatically opens and the game begins. Usually, you have no choice in where you sit, and the starting position of the button is decided at random.

If you play a lot of Sit & Go events on one site, you will soon get to know the regular players, on whom you will have notes. As most sites show you who is enrolled in any tournament before you have to pay your entry fee, you can look out for the names of players whom you want in your game or, possibly, to avoid.

Turbo Events

Some sites offer "Turbo" events, where the blinds rise every minute, or three minutes, or five minutes. These are, in effect, speeded up events and, as a result, they are far more of a gamble than a regular Sit & Go. If you must play them – presumably because you are impatient or in need of a brief thrill – then aggression, from the start, is essential. Ultimately, these quickie events come down to a crap-shoot. There's a lot of luck in poker, but this format relies on it way too much . . . so much so, it's almost not poker at all. So, the advice on Turbo events is simple: avoid them.

Sit & Go Strategy

Generally, Sit & Go events are marked by very aggressive play. It is neither a rare occurrence to find all-in bets within the first few minutes, nor to have one or more players eliminated after just a few hands. Because the style of Sit & Go events is now fairly well-established, better players have developed a strategy which gives them the best chance of finishing in the leading, money-winning positions. Let's examine this strategy now.

The two most important factors to remember for Sit & Go strategy are:

1. Players have only the chips in front of them. Once they have lost their stack, they're out. They cannot re-buy to replenish their stack. This makes a bet or call for all their chips much more significant; it makes the protection of your stack essential.

2. The event naturally breaks down into sections, or quartiles, during which different styles of play are usually correct. To alter those styles of play is called, in poker parlance, "changing gears" – and it is an essential element of successful tournament play.

The Four Quartiles of Sit & Go Events

I think that the best way to approach a Sit & Go event is to break it into four sections, or quartiles. The duration of each of these will depend on the format of the Sit & Go in which you are entered. This is something that you will learn to judge as you become more experienced. In simple terms, however, you might decide to consider each quartile as lasting 15-20 minutes.

Possibly the most significant element of each quartile is the relative value of your chip-stack to the blinds. For example, when you hold 1,000 chips and the blinds are 5/10, you have plenty of time to wait and fold. When your same 1,000 chips is facing blinds of 200/400 (towards the end of the event), clearly you are going to have to take action – and it is going to have to be dramatic.

First Quartile

This is the first few minutes of the tournament: use this time to study the style (and any notes) of the other players. Do not commit yourself to gambles and draws, keep raises small and be prepared to lay down any hand which is not a sure thing if there is a significant bet into you.

Certainly play premium hands, such as AA, KK, AK, QQ and JJ, and call cheaply any mid or low pair, hoping to spike trips, but do not chase hands; if the board brings overcards and opponents bet into you, throw away your pocket pair – it is not worth the risk to compete too far at this stage.

When raising, keep the initial pre-flop raise large, perhaps 5 or 6 times the big blind. Many players are very loose in the early stages of a Sit & Go (the exact opposite of the best long-term strategy) so small raises will find themselves being called all around the table. This bigger raise makes it more likely that you will face only one caller, and by reducing the field, you are protecting your premium hand.

Some players believe that the cheap blinds make this an ideal time to call loosely, hoping to hit a magic flop. If they stuck to that idea, it might be OK, but most players become tempted to call for draws when a partly promising flop hits (rather than the miracle one they told themselves they were playing for), and that is where chips can be drained away. For example, some experts like playing ace-low suited at this stage also, hoping to hit the nut flush. This is fine, so long as you muck your cards when there is anything other than an ultra-cheap draw after the flop.

To win a hand at this stage of the tournament is far less important and significant than to win hands at the later stages, when the pots will be much bigger and the pressure on all players will be greatest. To win one big pot in the third or fourth quartile of an event will be worth many, many smaller pots early on. I'm lazy; I'd rather win one big pot then toil over a dozen little, nerve-racking early ones.

So, during this first stage: play ultra-tight, be prepared to lay down to any confident betting by opponents, avoid bluffs which stand to pay little anyway, and gather information.

Second Quartile

This is the continuing early stage of the event. You have some idea of the style of your opponents and you can alter your own strategy slightly to oppose theirs. Be aware of players becoming short-stacked early on and look to take them on whenever you have a chance to do so, either with a strong starting hand, or having seen a relatively cheap flop. Keep in mind that these early short-stacks have been caused by hyper-activity early on and an element of desperation may have crept into their game already. Attack the short-stacks, but do so from a small beginning, to maximise your information from the flop and your opponent's reaction to it.

In terms of changing gears, in this stage, your observations will have led you to focus on certain opponents whom you will seek to attack, whereas you will remain tight and disciplined against others.

During these early stages (roughly half the event), your

betting decisions will be based entirely on your read of the deal in progress and your desire to maximise chip-building without taking any risks.

However, as you reach the second half of the event, your chip-stack – in relation to the size of the blinds – will begin to determine how aggressive you should become, and how soon.

Incidentally, it is amazing how often you can play no hands whatsoever and find yourself in the last four or five players. Most players are overly aggressive in the early stages and, although you will be facing a couple of players with big stacks, you will be there in the running without having done anything – and having given the impression of being ultra-tight. That is an impression that will only serve to help you during the third quartile.

Third Quartile
You may reach the second half of the Sit & Go with all the players still in their seats, or you may be in the money already. If it is the former, then the chip-stacks are likely to be reasonably balanced and the blinds are beginning to bite into people's stacks already. If you are one of only three or four players remaining, most of you will have decent stacks in relation to the blinds and you may have a little more time to be selective in your starting-hand choice.

Generally, however, this is the moment to start thinking: selective aggression. It is going to be your style for the rest of this quartile.

Attacking Short-Stacks
Be aware that a short-stack in this third quartile is far more vulnerable than in the first or second stages. This is because the blinds threaten to eat him up soon if he doesn't act. So, beware of pushing too hard against these players. If they feel that they have little to lose, they may well call you down and hope that they are best or that they catch a better hand. Players often raise or re-raise all-in, trying for a double through. Their

hands will almost certainly be sub-premium, but they only need to get lucky a couple of times to get right back into the event.

One key tactic is to lower your initial raise to ensure that you don't commit yourself to a hand or price yourself into a pot. For example, if you raise six times the big blind and a short-stack goes all-in, it will be hard for you to fold, even though you may be well behind. If you raise X3 instead and a short-stack goes all-in over you, you can get away from the hand (throw it away) without having damaged your own stack too badly.

Gear Changes and New Targets

You want to be seen as aggressive, but sensible. The best way to achieve this is to be raising or betting first. The simple reason here is that, to try to take you off the hand without a showdown (which all good players hate), an opponent probably knows it will take an all-in re-raise by him to make you consider laying down your hand. An all-in raise puts your opponent's entire tournament at risk and is not a measure he will want to take lightly.

To call your raise looks weak play and so opponents opt to fold rather than to become involved at all.

As the third quartile proceeds and the blinds rise even higher, choose your moments to bluff carefully. As discussed earlier, short-stacks may be too tempted to call you to make bluffing a reasonable policy. Equally, the chip leader may feel it worth the risk to call you down just on the off-chance that he can eliminate you from the event. So, it is the mid-range stacks you should attack now – the ones for whom the tournament is still wide open.

Short-Stack Tactics

Hopefully, you will have avoided becoming short-stacked, and you will still be hovering around average chips, with 10 blind rounds to last (that is, your stack can cope with 10 rounds of blinds before going bust – for example, if the blinds are 50/100, then you need 1,500 chips to feel relaxed and safe).

However, if through poor cards or poor luck you find yourself at 5 blind rounds or fewer, you must change gears immediately, become ultra-aggressive and seek to double up as soon as possible. Do not allow yourself to fall below this level or you will have no leverage against other players, nor will you have sufficient chips to make a double through a tournament-saving exercise.

In this situation, you must go all-in in late position (or in the blind positions if there has been no earlier raise).

All pocket pairs (high or low) should be bet with an all-in raise – in any position! Any hand that might reasonably be thought to be ahead should also be bet all-in: this will include ace-high hands, K10, KJ, etc. Do not be surprised to be called by poor hands also; opponents will be expecting you to make a last-ditch effort. However, often you will have a 40 per cent chance or better of doubling through and denting another opponent's stack. You must do this rather than allowing yourself to be blinded away. To go out of a tournament because the blinds have eaten you up is feeble.

Fourth Quartile

Let's imagine that you're down to the last four in a Sit & Go that pays the top three places. You've got above-average chips and you're feeling good. Do not allow yourself to be distracted. This is a key period in a Sit & Go. Most players tighten up at this stage, hoping that two other players will get into an all-in showdown and one will be eliminated, promoting everyone else into the money spots. This is the fight to avoid elimination "on the bubble" – the bubble being the last finishing spot which does not get paid.

Waiting around for something good to happen does work occasionally, but I urge you not to rely on it.

This will require courage, as it is the prime moment for a

racing gear-change to outright aggression. In this period you should seek to make all the action. If there is a pass or a check to you, you must bet, probably all-in, putting opponents on a decision for all their chips and, consequently, their tournament survival. Occasionally, you will run into pocket rockets or the like, or you may suffer an expected bad beat (eventually, something will click for an opponent) but you have a good chance of making several blind steals and re-raises to boost your stack. In other words, to be aggressive here wins out against all but the bravest, unless they pick up a huge hand in the hole.

Most opponents will curl up into defensive positions, folding and hoping desperately that someone else will crash out before them, and that gives you plenty of opportunity to build up the leading stack so that, even if you do get unlucky, you will still have chips left over to go at them a second time.

This strategy will result in you falling at this hurdle from time to time, but a fourth place finish – trying to win – is no dishonour. Fourth place, having been anted away, failing to make a stand – that would be shameful.

Crucially, this strategy, once you make it into the money, puts you in prime position to WIN the event, and not just claim third prize or rely on lucky gambling. Since first prize is always more than double and, sometimes, three times the value of third prize, this means that this strategy is a money-winning one also.

In the final minutes of a Sit & Go, all-in bets will be routine and, unless the blinds are still relatively low, an element of gambling creeps into each decision. The gamble is always better odds if you can get your money in first. Now, on top of the odds of winning the pot in the showdown, you also have the chance of your opponent folding with a poorer hand – and also with a better hand!

Heads-Up

As I hope you already know, the fewer the players at the table, the higher the value of any given hand. For example, whilst you would be unlikely to play K7 generally, when there are only three players remaining, this is a very playable hand; when you are heads-up, it is a very strong hand.

When you are down to the heads-up, again you may find you have a few moments to cherry-pick your hands while the blinds don't alter the relative chip-stacks too much. However, to lose even two big blinds in a row is likely to have some effect so, again, aggression, raising – probably all-in – is the winning strategy most of the time, even with moderate to half-decent poor hands.

Note also that, in a heads-up, every blind you win, not only boosts your stack, but depletes your opponent. So, at 300/600 blinds, when you take down the pot, you win a combined plus/minus pot of 1,800: 900 for you, 900 less for your opponent.

Watch out for the players who call almost everything down at this stage; possibly, now, you might wait for a half-decent starting hand. Most players, however, will wait – giving you vital blind collateral – until they have something meaty to call you with.

When you win – and, with a little luck and some steely determination, you will – take a moment to relish your success and then get serious again. Note down anything about your opponent's style when heads-up in case you meet him again. Ask yourself whether you played well and note what you did right and what you think you did wrong. Then, look for your next Sit & Go and continue making money.

Conclusion

Using your poker knowledge, adopting the standard strategy for online play, and following the strategy for Sit & Go events, you will find these (usually) one-table events very exciting. The action is fast and furious – keeping you focused – and the opportunity to make small profits over a long period of time is very achievable.

Our Sit & Go standard strategy is to:

• Avoid Turbo events.

• Be aware of the quartiles of the tournament.

• **In 1st quartile**: ultra-tight, no risk to your stack. Examine opponents' styles of play; aim to target weak/loose players later on; avoid all bluffs. Keep raises big (X5, X6).

• **In 2nd quartile**: loosen slightly, still do not risk all-in bets, don't bluff; keep raises big; be aware of your own chip-stack in relation to the size of blinds.

• **In 3rd quartile**: if short-stacked, shift to ultra-aggressive to regain momentum.

    If average-stacked, remain aware of relative stack size to blinds. Aim to attack mid-sized stacks: short-stacks may take any opportunity to get their chips into the pot to try for a double through.

    Reduce raise size to X2/X3 to allow for lay down if anyone threatening re-raises all-in after you.

    Remain especially aggressive if you have reached the bubble. Your aim is to steal chips from everyone by getting your chips into the pot first – make everyone else take the do-or-die decisions

• **In 4th quartile**: continue blind-stealing action aggressively. Be the first to take positive action whenever you can.

Remember that both the relative value of chips (compared to the blinds) and also the value of starting hands, has altered considerably since the event began.

- **In heads-up**: continue ultra-aggression, allow yourself time only if you have sufficient blinds to remain in control even if you surrender a few hands in a row.

- Remember to note heads-up opponent's style of play.

5

MULTI-TABLE TOURNAMENTS

A Multi-Table Tournament (MTT) is a brilliant way of going for the really big prize and perhaps encountering some of the big-name players out there (although you won't always know that you are playing them). The down side is that, unlike Sit & Go events, a Multi-Table Tournament is likely to have a field of hundreds, even thousands, and only the top 10 per cent or so get in the money. Even then, the real riches are reserved, quite rightly, for the final table. However, even reaching the final twenty or thirty players may give you your biggest poker pay-out of the year.

Online, MTTs are available twenty-four hours of the day. Look out for events with a "Guaranteed" prize-pot. That means that, even if there are insufficient players to make up the prize, the site will guarantee the advertised prizes. There may also be "Add-On Prize Pools", which is where a site adds on a certain amount (it might be $100, or $100,000) to whatever would be constituted by the entries alone.

Click on the MTT button in the lobby and you will be shown a list of the MTTs available and when they are scheduled to begin. Be aware of different time zones and ensure you know at what time the event will start, where you live.

Once you select an event, you can double-click on it to go to the "Tournament Lobby". There, you will see how to enter, how many players have enrolled, who they are, what the prize structure will be, and information such as the size of the blinds and how quickly they will escalate.

Once the tournament starts, the tournament lobby becomes a regularly updating thing of wonder. It shows you how many chips every player has, where you are in the ranking, who has been eliminated already, the exact prize money for each place. You can even watch another table in play. My advice is: look at this page during a break, and not while you're concentrating on your own table. Most MTTs feature a break, usually every hour or two. The break is usually 5 minutes, and all action is halted at the end of the hand in play.

Apart from entry fee and prize pool, you will also see that there are several different types of MTT. Some might play on tables of only six players, whilst most play on 8-, 9- or 10-player tables. Some may offer re-buys and add-ons.

Re-Buys
Some MTTs allow you to buy more chips if you get knocked out within the first hour (rarely, other time frames may be applied). After this re-buy period, once you lose your chips, you're out.

Be aware that MTTs which offer re-buys are likely to feature loose, aggressive play, right from the outset. This is because many players like to gamble early on, while they can still buy back into the event, to try to build a big chip-stack early on.

Note also that, after the re-buy period has expired, you are likely to experience an immediate tightening up of play at your table. You may be able to exploit this if you pick up some bluff and semi-bluff hands in good positions.

Should you re-buy? Not if you've just suffered a bad beat and your mind is scrambled, not if you think you're outclassed at your table. Yes, if you think you're up against players whom you can beat, and you feel confident and positive enough to develop your stack into a winning one.

Indeed, if you are going to enter an event with re-buys, I would budget for one re-buy. In this way, your decision whether to re-buy or not will be based, not on financial considerations, but on how you feel, how you rate your table, and whether you think you can make an impression on this event.

Add-Ons

Some MTTs allow you the opportunity to buy more chips at the end of a stated session (usually one hour, at the same time the chance to re-buy runs out). This allows you to top up your chips by adding on a fixed sum in exchange for some further entry money.

Should you add-on? Not if you're outclassed, tired, emotional or negative. And not if the add-on amount isn't sufficient to buy you plenty more rounds of blinds. If the blinds are already quite big, then an add-on may well not be worth the investment. However, usually, the add-on phase occurs while blinds are still low (although they are likely to rise directly the add-on period ends).

Generally, however, yes – add-on. You've entered the event to try to do well – having the most possible chips increases your chances of doing so. It shows your opponents that you are serious and confident about the tournament – and that is a good image to display.

If you can't afford the add-on, then maybe you shouldn't have entered the event in the first place – money should not be an issue here – you have more important things on which to concentrate.

Many players love these two additional twists to the traditional freeze-out event. They allow players extra chances to stay in the event and they boost the overall prize-pool, often considerably.

The down side is that they provide an excuse for wild and undisciplined play early on.

Satellites

Some MTTs may be satellites, in which you try to win – or sometimes finish within the top few places – to gain a seat in a bigger tournament for which you did not feel you could afford the entry fee.

For example, if you've set your heart on entering the annual $1,000 buy-in event on your site, you might try to qualify for it by entering a satellite for $100. In that event, for every ten entries, there would be a seat in the $1,000 main event up for grabs. If 100 players entered, there would be ten seats on offer to the players in the top ten (and it makes no difference if you are first or tenth, just that you are in the top ten).

If you didn't feel you could afford $100, you could enter a super-satellite for $10. If you qualified from that, you would now have a seat at the $100 satellite to try to qualify for the $1,000 event – and so on.

In the early twenty-first century, the majority of the field in the World Series of Poker final event qualified online, most of them through satellites and super-satellites. (The WSOP is the major series of live tournaments held in Las Vegas each summer. The "Big One" – the $10,000 buy-in NL Hold 'Em World Championship – is the culmination of five weeks of tournaments featuring the world's greatest players.) One year Chris Moneymaker took the top prize, having won his way through several super-satellites, satellites and the main event itself, all for the $39 it cost him to enter the first super-satellite.

Some super-satellites and satellites are one-table events – just like a Sit & Go – in which the winner wins a seat in the main MTT or into another, bigger, satellite. Others may be MTTs themselves where players who finish in the designated top places qualify for the main event or bigger satellite.

Be aware of the difference between having to win an event, or having to finish in, say, the top ten places.

In the former, you must be aggressive almost from the start – second place is no better than last. In the latter, you will adopt a pretty tight attitude throughout, picking your moment to strike with a premium hand or well-timed bluff. You do not want to risk your entire stack on a gamble. The preservation of your stack is paramount because, while it, and you, are still there, you might find yourself qualifying.

Often, as it gets close to the qualifying number of places, you can become a little more aggressive, to pick up blinds and put the decision-making emphasis on your opponents.

Many online sites offer satellites to live events, many televised, some in exotic settings, such as the WPT events in Aruba or Paris, others in the home of poker itself: Las Vegas. Most of these prizes are a package which includes flights and accommodation, so they are well worth winning.

MTT Strategy

Once you enter, or qualify for the main event, it's time to decide on how to approach what may be many hours of concentrated play.

The most important factors to remember for MTT strategy are:

1. In an event with no re-buys or add-ons, everyone is aware that they could go out on the next hand. Use that fear to intimidate opponents.

2. Tournaments which feature re-buys and add-ons usually start with aggressive, even wild, play as players try to increase their chip-stacks, unafraid of going bust, since they can buy back into the tournament.

3. There are quartiles to an MTT. Be aware of the passing time and remember to relate stack size to blind size; remain ready to change gears.

First Quartile

This first stage should be marked by a solid tightness from you, using the time to evaluate opponents at your table and decide against whom you can use your special skills.

Play premium hands strongly, raising big (X5, X6) to ensure that you reduce the number of callers and, therefore, protect your hand.

In late position, play promising suited connector hands (109s, J10s, etc.) but only remain in the pot if you pick up a straight flush draw, trips or 2-pair. In those cases, it will almost certainly be right to raise, once again, big – either to bully off or, at the very least, reduce the field against you.

You may also play ace-low suited, but only remain in pot for ultra-cheap flush draws. Do not chase pots when you hit aces, as your kicker will almost certainly cost you a packet.

The watchwords at the outset are: stack protection, information gleaning, solid image.

If you are playing with re-buys and add-ons – when the early stages are often filled with players gambling wildly to attempt an early strong start – you may simply choose to pursue the above strategy, perhaps calling down a few more hands if you strongly suspect wild bluffing from your opponent. Because the general table style will be much looser and more aggressive, you may well be able to slow play your way to some big pots, since your opponent may raise for you each time.

You may choose to join in the throng and get bullying yourself, trying to steal pots and compel others to gamble against you. However wild you choose to be, stay aggressive. That is to say, cancel the tight hand selection element of your standard strategy tight/aggressive style, but still play and bet every hand aggressively like it was a premium one. You have so many more chances to win if you are raising, whether or not you have a hand.

If you enjoy that style, be prepared to re-buy several times, but also, on occasion, to go into the next stages of the tournament with a significant stack of chips, giving you both waiting time and bullying power.

Second Quartile

Unless you are already short-stacked, in which case you must change gears and become much more aggressive immediately, the second quartile should see a slow increase in looser hand selection, but similar aggression in betting style.

You should have some basic knowledge of each of the players at your table (and have taken some notes) and you must use that to help you to make the right plays at the right time, against the right person. Have the courage to form a picture of what is happening on any given hand and, if you believe you can take the pot, bet at it. Even if you go wrong sometimes, this will help you to develop a feel for playing hands at the right moment.

Bluffs should be kept to a minimum, and any pot that risks all, or a significant proportion, of your chips should be laid down. You are still appearing to behave as a tight/aggressive player and that is definitely the image that you are happy to project right now.

Table Personnel

Remain aware that in MTTs, until you reach the final table when players from your table are eliminated, players will soon be replaced by new players. Focus on them if you can and glean as much as you can about their playing style as quickly as possible.

You sometimes find that your entire table disappears and players are dispersed throughout the event onto new tables. This is frustrating, but it is part of playing in any big Multi-Table Tournament. Regroup as quickly as you can, take notes on new opponents, and attack short-stacks most keenly.

Third Quartile

If you are here, you are at the meat of the tournament. However, just because you've made it this far, it does not mean that you can relax. Far from it. Now is the time to get moving. You must become more aggressive pre-flop and hope that your earlier "tight" image buys you some blinds and called bets. Use that impetus to bully the short- and mid-short stacks by using all-in bets against those players who hold fewer chips than you. This is the time to use the all-in move against these players just hanging in there, hoping they might just squeeze into the money. Use it, pre-flop, on all pairs, AK, AQ, etc., as well as post-flop on made hands and good drawing hands.

You have to remain aggressive here to counter the tightness that tends to occur as the bubble approaches. Use your opponents' feelings of vulnerability and fear to bolster your own stack by betting big. Steal blinds and make players gamble; many will just fold quietly.

You may lose those gambles (although the odds are certainly in your favour) but, if you do not force the issue, your chip-stack will dwindle anyway, and you will be blinded away, before you hit the money.

As with Sit & Go, you may find yourself eliminated a few places short of the bubble but, if you make it through, you will be well ahead of the bubble and in the running for a final table position. That should always be your aim, both economically (the final table prizes are many, many times the value of those just inside the bubble), and also psychologically, since to win the event could mean a life-changing sum of money.

Blinds and Ante Bets

Be aware that in many big MTTs, as well as rising blinds, by the latter half of the third quartile there may also be ante bets deducted on every hand. To start, you may find that, say, 100 of your chips are placed in the middle along with the blind bets. Even if the ante bets taken from every player on every hand start small, they will rise with the blinds. This means that every hand that is played is costing you chips. Pay attention to how they affect the length of time you have left before you must commit yourself to doubling-up to get back into the tournament. Do not delay that decision too long, or your double-up will not be sufficient to protect you.

Avoid Becoming Short-Stacked

There is a huge pile of luck, as well as skill and judgment, that goes into tournament success. You want to rely on that luck as little as possible. However, when you are short-stacked, you must rely on either a great starting hand, or hitting something on the board. As ever, the aggressive, all-in approach offers you the extra chance of everyone folding to you, and that is why to work – to minimise the luck – you must go all-in soon after you realise that you must take action. Do not allow yourself to become short-stacked. Before that time comes, go for an all-in move and try to double through. The top players never allow themselves to be anteed or blinded away. They always go down fighting (and, with a little good timing, often come back up to finish well in the money).

Fourth Quartile

If you are here, you are close to the final table. If you are very short-stacked and you've just scraped in, then pick any decent hand and get all your chips into the middle as soon as you can. If you can double through now, twice, you are right back in the race. If not, forget it. Unless the prize money goes up hugely between, say, 19th and 18th places, just stay ultra-aggressive and hope to get lucky. Try to go all-in when you are not in the blinds; this means that you have both blinds to pick up if you can force a fold. Never get blinded away.

If you are mid-stacked, then remain alert and aggressive. There is a new "bubble" approaching, and it's called the final table. As with all bubbles, whether they be at Sit & Go, or the first prize-money bubble, many players tighten up as they approach these poker landmarks. To reach the final table in a big event will have taken hours, will usually pay well, and offers the chance still of winning the whole tournament. For this reason, stay aggressive; you have a good chance of forcing opponents into folding. Keep observing who is short-stacked, who is desperate, and who is just trying to coast higher up the rankings without taking any risks. Use that knowledge to attack each player in the appropriate way.

Final Table

You've made it to the final table. Congratulations. You are tired after many hours of play, and delighted to reach that hallowed poker space.

Don't panic. It's just a big Sit & Go really, and you know how to play those. Don't wander off to tell anyone you can find that you've made it, because the game usually continues until the scheduled break.

Check the Pay Schedule

Check your stack against everybody else, check your stack against the blinds, take a quick note of the prize money for each place and make some decisions... Depending on how you are doing, you must set yourself a target and play for it.

If the difference between 10th and 6th is $5,000, you may feel that you just want to hang in there while a couple more players get knocked out. If the difference is much less, but the top three places are paid really well, then perhaps aim for them and don't get worried if you get knocked out first rather than later on.

Finally, of course, you want to get heads-up with one opponent, get lucky and play shrewdly, and take all his chips. If that's your aim, then remain very aggressive and go for it. Calling and checking won't win you this thing. Get your finger on the raise button, watch out for your position and relative chip-stacks, and play hard and with total conviction.

If you make it to heads-up, remember that your hand values increase hugely. Any ace is very big, a pair huge, and suited connectors promising. The winning hand will likely be very low, possibly even just a high card.

If the blinds are low, take a little time to learn your

opponent's strategy and try to beat him at it, selecting hands carefully. If you are ahead, keep raises small so that you don't become pot-committed. This is the worst of all times to double an opponent's stack.

If you are behind, then you must be the aggressor as often as possible. Bully, nag and outwit your opponent into giving you more chips.

If the blinds are high, then almost any hand could pot-commit you. You must pick a decent one and push all your chips in. This will be a battle of nerve and, when the nerve breaks, luck. But, if you have more chips than your opponent because you've bullied him up to the time he calls you down, you can afford the gamble, and he can't!

Finally, a word about playing someone against whom you believe you are outclassed. The answer is: try to make him gamble. If you slow play him, he'll outplay you. Pick your hands, push all-in – probably pre-flop, and watch him squirm.

Conclusion

Using your poker knowledge, adopting the standard strategy for online play, and following the strategy for MTTs, you will give yourself a real chance of placing in an MTT and winning significant sums of money.

However – a warning. These events are not for the faint-hearted. Even the world's best players can play dozens of tournaments, both online and live, and not make the big money. You can play online for four or five hours and then just miss out on the prizes – then it feels like a big waste of time. You can make the money and about to double through and head for the final table, when a bad beat strikes. This happens every minute of every day and it will happen to you too. However, once you gain the confidence to play aggressively, you will find yourself in the running with a chance at a big jackpot.

The chances of winning, especially if it is early in your poker-playing career, are relatively small, but it can be done and, when it is, the rewards are big, both financially and psychologically, in terms of the huge boost in confidence a win will provide.

This standard strategy gives you the benchmarks of successful basic play and allows you to use your own talents to add to your chip-stack.

Our MTT standard strategy – very similar to our Sit & Go strategy – is to:

- Avoid Turbo events.

- Be aware of the quartiles of the tournament.

- Take notes on players whenever you have the chance. Build your MTT database of information on all possible opponents.

- **In 1st quartile**: ultra-tight in early and mid position; play suited connectors, all pairs, ace-small in late position – do not risk your stack on any bluff or semi-bluff except perhaps straight flush draws.

- Examine opponents' styles of play; aim to target weak/loose players later on; avoid all bluffs.

- Keep raises big (X5, X6).

- In MTTs with re-buys and add-ons, be aware of likely aggression and wildness from some players. Consider calling down those players to expose bluffs. You may choose also to adopt a similar reckless approach, trying to build a stack, whilst still having opportunities to buy back into the tournament.

- **In 2nd quartile**: loosen slightly, risk all-in bets only against shorter stacks and when your hand, or pressure, makes it likely that you will win either by bluffing or at showdown. Avoid all bluffing and against-odds drawing when facing the chip leader or big stack. Keep raises big; be aware of your own chip-stack in relation to the size of blinds.

- **In 3rd quartile**: if short-stacked, shift to ultra-aggressive to regain momentum. If average-stacked, remain aware of relative stack size to blinds. Aim to attack mid-sized stacks: short-stacks may take any opportunity to get their chips into the pot to try for a double through.

- Reduce raise size to X2, X3 to allow for lay down if anyone threatening re-raises all-in after you.

- Remain especially aggressive if you have reached the bubble. Your aim is to steal chips from everyone by getting your chips into the pot first – make everyone else take the do-or-die decisions.

- **In 4th quartile**: continue blind-stealing action aggressively. Be the first to take positive action whenever you can. Remember that both the relative value of chips (compared to the blinds) and also the value of starting hands have altered considerably since the event began.

- **At final table**: set goals for yourself and play for those. To win, you must remain aggressive at all times.

- **In heads-up**: continue ultra-aggression, allow yourself time only if you have sufficient blinds to remain in control even if you surrender a few hands in a row.

6

BAD BEATS AND DEVELOPING A POKER TEMPERAMENT

A "bad beat" is a situation where your hand has a significant statistical advantage before the arrival of one, two, or all five, of the communal cards on the board, but your opponent then overtakes your hand to take the pot. Note this: ". . . you have a **significant** statistical advantage . . ."

Assuming an average level of poker ability and under-standing, there is nothing in the game which will affect your overall results – be they in cash games, Sit & Go events or MTTs – more than your poker temperament. Dealing with highs is usually easy; it is the lows which will affect you and your bankroll significantly.

Millions of people play poker worldwide, and they have no idea how to control their emotions at the table, be it in a live game or online. If you can master what is in this chapter, you will lose much less, win more, and feel great doing it. To ignore this section, to believe that it is esoteric and somehow not appli-cable to you, will be to ruin all your efforts in improving your strategies. I would argue that more money is lost through poor poker temperament than through poor poker play.

This happened to me while I was preparing to write this section:

I'm playing a $100 buy-in tournament and I'm doing well. A player raises mid position with A10, and I re-raise all-in with AKs. The player calls, and the flop comes 10108. That's half my stack gone.

Ten minutes later, a player raises mid position with 55. I re-raise with AA, doubling his bet; he goes all-in and I call. The flop comes K85 . . . and does not improve. That's me out.

Both these beats occurred in an MTT with a relatively small buy-in. These bad beats occur more frequently in low-limit tourneys and cash games because the style of play is almost always too loose; the players are usually quite weak also but, most significantly, they are gamblers. I doubt that such bets would be made by stronger players in higher limit games and it is clearly noticeable that, in the higher value games, players' respect raises a little more and, generally, they are far less inclined to gamble all the chips on a real (and, almost certainly, odds against) gamble. Tough as they are, you have to get used to them.

To suffer two such beats within fifteen minutes would be very unlucky in a live game and would, quite possibly, wipe out your stake, or eliminate you from the tournament. Online, because you play so many hands per hour, that does happen and it happens regularly, especially when you are playing against weak opponents. The expectation for such a series of bad beats becomes far greater than normal. You must get used to this and reserve only the briefest of moments for regret and frustration. You must focus on the fact that you got your money into the pot when you were a clear statistical favourite. Keep doing that and you WILL win, even if, perhaps for prolonged periods, it seems as if the odds are not conforming.

By the way, neither of my bad beats was particularly bad. AKs does indeed dominate A10, but, in fact, it is only 73 per cent on to win, plus 4.5 per cent or thereabouts for a split pot. So, roughly 3-1 on isn't as strong as it might seem. AA v 55 seems even worse and it is – a little. The Rockets are 80 per cent on to win, so at roughly 4-1, it's a shame that a feeble 55 overtook me, but it's not majorly unlucky.

In both cases, what was annoying was that neither player should have stuck his/her chips into the pot when they did. However, you want players to make mistakes and put their money in when you are behind because, if they didn't do that, you would have to get lucky to beat them. So, when they do make a mistake, enjoy it – even if ultimately, the luck of the deck makes them overtake you. In the long run, that won't happen.

Incidentally, a few years back, to crash out of an MTT like that would have put up my blood pressure, caused me to howl for a few minutes and probably bang my desk/shout at the dog/stomp up and down the room. Then, I would open up a few more tables and play "on tilt" – out of control, seeking revenge, angry at the world. These days, it still annoys me, but the negative emotion passes quickly.

Analysis of Bad Beats
If the number of bad beats you seem to be receiving seems very high to you, then take note of these hands to study at the end of a session. At the very least, this will either reassure you that you got your money in at the right moments – or expose that you misplayed or misjudged a series of hands. Indeed, you may even discover that these so-called "bad beats" were actually much closer propositions than you first imagined.

Just take a note of the hand on which they occurred and study the hand records at the end of the session.

The fact is that because something is statistically likely to occur 60 per cent of the time, if you take 100 examples of this situation at the poker table (and that might be over several sessions, over several weeks or even months), the likely variation from expectation will be very high: you might easily win 90 per cent of those hands, or perhaps only 30 per cent of them. Increase that to 1,000 hands, and the range is very likely (but not guaranteed) to be closer to the expected 60 per cent –

perhaps the range is now 50-70 per cent. Move to 100,000 examples, and the actual success rate will move closer to the expected range, let's say 58-62 per cent. However, for any given situation at poker, to conform very closely to the expectation, it might take years or even decades worth of playing.

As a result, by the time you have played a lifetime of poker, the expectation and the resultant percentage are very close and here, in this example, even if you are at the lower end of the range, you are still well in profit. That is no comfort to you when you're in the middle of a six-month bad run but, unless you are the one-in-the-million player who defies the odds over many thousands of hands (and, statistically, there must be some like that), you will come good.

Aftermath

The real danger of bad beats is not that they defy the odds – that is merely part of the expectation – but that they affect your mental state as you move on into subsequent hands. For example: following a bad beat, you raise one from the button with AJ and the big blind re-raises you. Usually, you should fold now but it's easy to feel that everything is moving against you, so you re-raise all-in and find that you are facing QQ, KK, maybe AK or even, in a loose game, AQ. Any of those hands puts you down as a substantial dog – and it's your fault. Such a play is likely to wipe out whatever stake you have remaining, or eliminate you from the event. I have seen, time and time again, more money lost on the bad beat REACTION than on the beat itself.

Bad beats are tough mentally, particularly if you have read the hand correctly and put your money in at the right moment, but they are a fact of poker. Also a fact is that truly bad beats happen far less often than we might care to believe. If you bet the top pair on the flop, and a player re-raises all-in for a flush draw with two overcards and you call, and then you go on to lose, that isn't a bad beat – the player had 15 out cards against you: 9 for the flush, 6 for pairing his overcards – that represented a 54 per cent chance of you being beaten. So, he was ahead and YOU were the underdog. Even if the player has one overcard to your top pair, he has 12 outs or 45 per cent with two cards to come. Again, if he hits his hand, this is no bad beat. Indeed, you should question whether you should be risking all your chips, even a big bet, on a 45 per cent chance. You could, and should, be looking for better odds to pile your chips into the middle – either metaphorically or literally.

By the way, straight after I had been eliminated from that tournament, I decided to play a little cash game – just $2/$4 NL Hold 'Em. After about ten minutes, I raise in first position with AA, and I get called by five players. Yes, count them – five players! Already my heart is sinking, because, as we discussed, multiple callers weaken your hand.

The flop comes K72, the latter two cards being spades. Rightly or wrongly, I decide to put in a big bet – $100 – just over the size of the pot. Everyone folds except the second guy who had called my raise.

He goes all-in for another $370. So what does he have?

As a reader, you cannot really work this out without knowing a bit about the player. I didn't have any notes on him, and I hadn't noticed anything about his play in the dozen or so hands we had played since I joined the table. I'm not even sure he had been in many hands. I guess you have to put him on 77, giving him trips, but he could also be on A♠ and another ♠ I guess.

I think for a while and, despite my read that he held 77, I decide to call. This non sequitur, I concede now, was partly inspired by my untimely exit from the tournament. However, my call is right: he has 106 of spades, so he needs to hit his 35 per cent flush draw and I am correct to get my money in . . . Needless to say, he hits a spade on the turn and that's the end of me.

This result is bad enough but, what on earth was he doing calling a big first position raise on 106? I could feel my blood boiling and I could hear myself muttering (that's always a bad sign). I left the table and logged off the site.

So, I reflected, I was well ahead each time I got my money into the pot, several times the other player shouldn't even have been in the hand, and each time I lost. That made me even more angry and now, thanks to many years of such things, this reaction caused me not to carry on in the game, trying to chase my money back from this "ignorant fool", but instead to stop playing for a while.

Talking About Bad Beats

Perhaps you speed-read those last paragraphs? The fact is that everyone suffers bad beats – or what they think are bad beats – every session they play and it is natural to want to talk about them in an attempt to elicit sympathy. The problem is that no one really wants to hear your stories, so you don't get the sympathy and reassurance you were seeking, and that makes you even more angry, self-pitying and resentful.

Everyone suffers them, everyone believes theirs is the worst ever, and no one really enjoys hearing about them. If you can – and this is easier said than done – try not to talk about them at all. If you must (and all of us get the urge sometimes) then keep the story short and don't expect too much sympathy. When others tell you about their beats, try not to get even with them by telling them one of your own. Just give them a few moments of understanding, a hug, a pat on the shoulder and move on. Once your friends know that you are only good for a few moments of time for their stories, they'll start to keep theirs shorter too.

A side effect of this is also mental. The less you talk about them, the less the event and the aftermath will play on your mind. Gradually, you will condition yourself to take the beat and move on and the effect on your attitude to future hands will be greatly improved.

I have seen online players – good ones too – playing four tables simultaneously. They take a bad beat on two of those tables in quick succession and then their game collapses for a few minutes. When you're playing four tables, it can lead to VERY costly mistakes. When you're watching what your opponents are doing at your own table, seeing whether they are playing at other tables too, this can benefit you hugely if you're around with the right cards at the right time to exploit them.

Reaction to Bad Beats

How you react to a bad beat, or a sequence of them, will contribute hugely to the size of your bankroll at the end of every session you play.

1. If you can truly say that you are unaffected by bad beats, then that is a great talent. Even if it takes you a hand or two to recover, that is still great going. Sit out a hand, or two hands – and then rejoin the game.

2. If, like me, you are still unsettled by bad beats (especially when the player should never have still been in the hand) then a particularly loathsome beat, or series of bad beats, should be met by this simple action:

    Log off the table . . . Preferably log off the site altogether. Take a walk, make a cup of tea or coffee – take a break for a few minutes. Remind yourself that the player did what you wanted him to: he put his money in when the odds were WELL against him – he just got lucky.

3. However, if like many poker players, a bad beat affects your game for hours afterwards then, to protect yourself and your bankroll, you must train yourself to stop playing poker for the day. Just stop.

I suspect that, as soon as we have a basic understanding of the game, we all start out in category 3, and slowly train ourselves to survive in category 2.

However, category 2 means stopping playing for a short period of time, the moment you feel your emotions beginning to enter your thoughts even for a moment. That takes discipline, but it will be rewarded by actual money – winnings – at the end of a period of play, since you will not have played in unfavourable conditions where you would be likely to lose. To take a break saves money and it protects your hard-won self-confidence at the poker table.

The really important thing about bad beats is this: you need to suffer them if you are going to be a winning poker player!

If we can discipline our minds sufficiently to appreciate that the situation in which bad beats occur is exactly the situation that we seek, that we need to see (opponents have their money in the pot against us, when the odds of their winning are poor), then we will realise that we cannot win at poker without leaving ourselves open to the possibilities of bad beats. Indeed, the more real bad beats we suffer, the better we are playing and the more – in the long run – we will win. However, that can be tough after days and weeks of being overtaken by the turn and river cards.

If you keep notes of your sessions, marking where you think bad beats occurred, then at least you will be able to review these notes to check whether the beat really was bad, and how your session went after the bad beat (or beats). If you find that your session is negatively affected by bad beats, then you must take action to avoid this becoming a repeated feature of your games.

So, to conclude – and to repeat – strange as it may be: you WANT to suffer bad beats. If your opponents do not put their money into a pot when you are ahead, when you are likely to win, then winning will be very tough indeed.

7

A MISCELLANY OF TIPS AND
STRATEGIES FOR
ONLINE POKER

This is a selection of tips and advice for online poker – indeed poker generally. Dip into them from time to time to inspire yourself to ever greater successes at the poker table, be it when playing in home games, live cash games, tournaments or online.

Patience, Patience, Patience

Online poker should help you to play tighter. There may be impatient aspects of your game (which may manifest themselves in a live game) such as: playing only a small number of hands per hour; being aware of a finite amount of time to play because you are in a club, casino or private home; frustration at being stuck at a table you do not like and at which you seem unable to make headway. All these frustrations should melt away in online play. At least double the hands per hour will be dealt, you can play for as long as you like, and you can switch tables, change stakes dramatically, or move to a fast-action tournament table.

Use this faster pace and wider set of options, not to speed up your own game, but to become more disciplined and less stressed about runs of bad cards, or matters not turning out as you wish them to: there is another hand seconds away, another table available, other people against whom to test your skills.

As well as frustration, which is a major money-loser, tiredness is a catalyst for losing play. When playing online, you know that there will still be games when you've taken forty winks, or you wake in the morning. Use this knowledge to, metaphorically, stand up from the table and call it a day – at least for a while.

Pick Your Times

The time of day for you to play is the one during which you feel most alert and focused and are least likely to be disturbed. Try to turn off mobile phones, noisy children, and general disturbance. Do not try to play while you get on with menial tasks. It's tempting, but you will lose an edge if you are not constantly observing your opponents.

If you can, search out poker sites which are global. This may offer you the opportunity of playing against opponents from a different time zone.

For example, if you play in the UK, to have a session in the morning may work very well if you can play against players from the United States. These people may have been playing all night and are either cash-happy with their winnings or chasing their losses after a long, frustrating, bad session.

In the afternoon or evenings, you might want Far-Eastern or Australasian opponents for similar reasons because they may have been playing for six, eight, ten hours longer than you.

There are sites which are based in, or specifically cater for, different countries, and many which offer alternative currencies in which to play. The simple mechanics of asking people where they are is friendly, but it is also useful information to you and should be added to any notes you take about them.

Taking on tired, drained players is a fine way to demonstrate your disciplines and your poker skills to result in significant online profits.

Observations and Tells

Online poker requires just the same observational skills as a live game when it comes to noticing betting patterns or styles, even though you are deprived of the physical presence of your opponent(s). Such styles should be noted wherever possible.

Within the context of such actions, there are still plenty of "tells" to watch for. As you play more, you will begin to notice these increasingly and, in turn, you will gain a new reading skill when it comes to live games, which is one reason why online players have been doing so well in live tournaments:

Automatic Check

When players have pressed the "Check/Fold" button, the instantaneous check by the computer, particularly in the big blind position, indicates disinterest in the hand. Small blinds who call and see the instant check can pretty safely bet the flop if any high cards appear, but be particularly wary should the flop come, say 772, when the big blind may now just have flopped the nuts.

Similarly, if the Check/Fold option is often chosen by the big blind player, it will be worth making a minimum raise in the small blind position – provided that there are no other callers – simply to see the hand automatically folded. Even if this only works 50 per cent of the time, for the remaining 50 per cent you still have the advantage of having shown strength, and you may well be able to take down the pot on the flop.

Similar positions occur on all rounds of betting following the flop. It is amazing to me how many players will indicate their complete lack of interest in a hand they have called for the moment the flop hits the board. This is equivalent to the, usually inadvertent, shrug or shoulder slump, in the live game. The reason for their behaviour: frustration, impatience.

Quick Check
It will be profitable to get into the habit of ensuring that you hesitate every time the action moves to you (say, five to ten seconds). While some players may consider this a tell, for a less experienced player it will serve to standardise your reaction times and hide when you are thinking and when you have missed the flop and subsequent cards. To check quickly after the flop (and early in subsequent rounds) indicates a lack of any consideration for the deal. This signals to your opponents that you are not a concern and that they can eliminate you from any calculations they may be making about how much to bet or raise, knowing that you will not be a factor.

Final Bet Hesitation
This usually occurs on the final round of betting and is usually easy enough to smoke out. A drawing player hits his straight or flush or even trips the bottom pair on which he has called you down, and now wants to appear as if he's bluffing with a big bet, often an all-in. Players may wait until the last second to stick in all their chips. You may find yourself calling these to begin with but, for the vast majority of the time, these hesitations are merely a feeble attempt to paint a false picture.

If you find yourself at a table with several such players, occasionally consider such a play yourself, but when you have missed your draw. Your opponents will think that they know what is happening because it is the play they routinely make with the Nuts. You, however, have saved it for a far more opportune and, inevitably, difficult position for them to read.

Ego

You are playing in a low-stake game to bolster your bankroll or to build up courage and you know that you are the best player, or among the best, at the table. Do not expect the results to follow your perceived form or train of thought quickly. Bad players can get lucky for long periods of time; the cards can go dead on you. Even a four-hour session online is subject to massive swings.

The danger is that you try to steam through your opponents as if this was tournament play. You catch a couple of poorish beats, and reload the small maximum. It happens again (and possibly again and again after that). You leave the low-stake game, disgusted at the looseness and poor betting shown by the weaker players. You return to your own game and you are still steaming. You start to raise more than usual to assert yourself. A few raises get called and beat you. Now, you're really steaming – and your chips slide away, relentlessly.

Your plan should be long term, your session results of only marginal importance. Make it a professional discipline not to allow a session to get the better of you. More bad sessions are caused by you, yourself, than ever by your opponents or the turn of the cards.

The original "poker brat", Phil Hellmuth Junior, quite rightly observes that decent players are often arrogant about their ability against players whom they perceive to be weak. You can't just beat a player because he is weak, you have to outplay him. Respect him, tease out of him what his weaknesses actually are, and then set a trap for him – or let him trap himself.

First Hands

The early play at your first table of a session is important, both financially and psychologically. You should get used to altering your play accordingly.

To start a session losing a big hand, or several medium-sized ones, means that part of your mind is on catch-up. With a maximum bankroll, this is lessened but it is still there. Contrast this with the feeling that you get when you are playing with your opponents' money. I'm sure that you immediately appreciate that this is when your mind is freed up and positive. This always results in optimum play (provided that over-confidence/ego does not take over).

There is another vital factor: information. You have new opponents, on some of whom hopefully you have notes. Otherwise, you have had only a little time to observe their styles and moods. Such knowledge will influence your tactics, bets and playing style in due course, so do not allow yourself to be conned into hands in which you will be forced to make big decisions with the minimum amount of information available. If in doubt, take a passive route. Increase your standards for calling and raising and sit back – to learn. You may even succeed in representing yourself as a tight pushover. Then, a few minutes later, with opponents firing at you, you can start hitting them with serious re-raises.

Weak Games are not Easy Games
To play in a game of beginners or, seemingly better yet, players who think they are tremendous and in fact are very poor, sounds like a licence to print money. But, beware. Such games have some very serious flaws from your point of view:

• Bluffing simply may not be available – weak players tend to call down hands on a whim.

• The all-in bet or raise will be applied far more often (and, just because they are poor players does not mean that they can't afford to lose the tiny stakes they are playing, over and over again). This leaves you gambling rather then allowing your superiority slowly to grind you into profit, hand by hand.

- Your big hands may be called by too many players. Ultimately, profits in very weak games often go to those who hold the best cards after the river! Because so many people play the flop in weak games, your AA may look great but when you raise and get four callers, you are now odds against to win the hand.

The solution, dull though it is, is to tighten up and play ultra-tight/aggressive style: folding endlessly until you hit a truly big hand – possibly after the flop – and then betting huge. Here's your edge coming now: such a policy will not win against good players, but at this weak table you are much more likely to get a caller – and one with the wrong type of hand. That's when you make your money. It's not much fun, this style, but it will make you money.

Resentment

To personalise your opponent in a live game is very much understandable. Online, however, there is no excuse. As discussed in Chapter 1, using the chat box is not recommended. It is not a wise method of excreting your negative emotions, since it reveals them to all the table, but it is also a conduit through which some players may try to personalise themselves in order to manipulate you. I have heard recounted tales of players telling stories about being in debt, living in a bed-sit, breaking up with their partners, their children sick – simply to elicit sympathy and alter their opponents' mind-sets when it came to betting against them.

Even if you engage in the briefest of exchanges with opponents, there is the chance to get into a discussion or an argument. Poker is very much a game of judgment, and, as there are so many judgments to discuss, conflict is inevitable. If you engage in this conflict, even witness it, it will affect the way you are thinking – and you must not let this happen.

Finally, the resentment which slowly builds when you feel that you are being outplayed by an inferior player, or you are watching everyone else enjoying hands with a fat cash-cow, spewing chips, and you are seeing nothing but 73 and 92 off, will boil over if you are in conversation – it is the natural thing to do. Resist this, because it will only make your resentment grow. Disengage with any notion you may have that your opponents are people. They are just opponents, and you must have greater control over your own mind, than they have over theirs.

On a similar note, if you are in a bad mood today, don't play. You may rationalise by telling yourself that you deserve some downtime, a chance to escape the endless frustrations of the real world, but the poker table is not the place to do it. Ask any decent player you know and he will tell you that his poor sessions tend to match his own poor moods.

More than that, if you have a bad day and follow it up with a few bad sessions at the poker tables, you will start to get paranoid and then your poker results really will suffer. Take a break and play the next day. It's discipline again, I'm afraid.

De-Humanisation
Being a decent type, you hate to kick a man when he's down; a worthy value – but 100 per cent out of place at the poker table.

Poker is a mental combat sport; people will get injured. You will be among them from time to time. But no one is compelled to remain at the table, taking a beating. There is no shame attached to leaving the game – particularly online – taking a short break and rejoining another game (even the same one, if you truly think it's a really good one for you). For that reason, you must be merciless at the table. Put aside thoughts of humanity for a while: this is a game and, within it, you are allowed to bully, intimidate and generally rough up your opponents. When a live game ends, that is the time to express your sympathy. Online, that time never comes; you just take your profit and move on.

You may instinctively feel that this makes poker sound like

an unfriendly game. It should not. You will get respect from everyone who is truly interested in poker as a skill. Poker friendships are often very strong and trusting, but they never develop from one player taking mercy on another at the table. If you feel that guilty, put a percentage of your annual winnings into a charity box – it'll be a good-sized donation.

Marginal Hands

As we develop as poker players, we go through phases of trying to find the style of play which suits us best. Inevitably, there will be a period of time in every player's life when he plays loosely and unpredictably. Some keep going and make millions (like Gus Hansen, Phil Ivey and Daniel Negreanu, although you have to be brilliant to do it – as these three are) but, generally, you make a tighter style your default mode of operation.

However, during this loose phase, we notice that when we call raises with low suited-connectors, or call early with QJ off, we do win pots, and some of them are huge. The problem is that our brains emphasise these winning occasions and repress the multiple boring occasions when we end up folding. The result is that we start to play marginal hands without even realising how marginal they really are. Our win rate falls and we blame it on our cards.

Until I read and thought about marginal hands in this following way, I found it difficult to focus on laying them down. Every pair of hole cards can be rated with a percentage win/loss figure over a lifetime. As usual, big anomalies may occur in the short term (when the flop keeps hitting you perfectly) but, eventually, your own stats will approach the predicted outcome.

So, if you take a hand like Q8 off played in all positions, you might find that after five years of play you have won $10,000, but lost $40,000. Think of it this way: every time you play Q8 off, you are spending 25c per dollar you bet. That's 25 per cent! Slot machines in Vegas take, maybe, 5-10 per cent and they have made casino owners billions of dollars, consistently over the decades. Ask yourself? Am I that much of a sucker?

Solid Play – The Psychological Problem

You may find yourself following the guidelines in this book, using your own poker skills fully, and still you lose. You lose and lose and lose.

You must have the courage not to change your winning style and allow what are probably quite small losses to affect the way you approach the game. Everyone else may be having fun for now, but you will be sitting on profits, long term, and you can be magnanimous enough to let them enjoy themselves for a while. The recommended style here will mean that you win in the long term, and you must stick to it – even if it is hurting badly for now. This will fly in the face of your instinct; you must get it under control.

If You are Going to Call, Bet or Raise First

Since even experienced players forget this general rule, it is worth repeating because it goes towards characterising your image at the table.

If you bet, rather than call, you come across as a positive, confident, value-grabbing player. This will, in due course, affect the way players react to your bets and raises. Almost imperceptibly, your opponents will start to call less, knowing that they will so frequently face further bets from you at every turn. Over time, the effect for you will be cumulative wins from bets and raises, allowing you to steal more small pots.

Picking Your Spot

Waiting only for great hands and capitalising on them is only one part of a solid, winning online game.

What players call "Picking your spot" is another vital area. You are familiar with your opponents' styles of play, you have notes on most, you are alert to the rhythms of the play and you suddenly sense an opportunity: to run a bluff, to slow play, to button raise, to blast out the opposition. This is "picking your spot" – and it is only achievable if you are fully focused on your game. Missing these chances is just as costly as mistakenly folding your pocket rockets.

Cards Get Better-Looking the Fewer You See

When you've had an hour or two of no action, particularly since online there is usually action all over the place, your marginal hands start looking big. I've stared longingly at K8 suited sometimes and thought it looked sexy. It's not. It'll lose you money in the long run. Every time you pass a hand like that, you're saving yourself money.

Remember that it is easy to be disciplined and professional when you are winning, but you must sustain that professionalism even when the going is very dull. As oft stated previously, if you want to have fun, don't play online poker to win. However, if you can learn to use this relative downtime to study your opponents, look at hand records and observe betting styles, then the cards will change and you will be in a position to return to winning. Since every loss saved will increase your profit, this attitude to play is essential to your success.

Can't Wait to Play?

Nor can I.

For me, it's the same with golf in the summer. But . . . I've learnt that the more eager I am to play, the faster I swing, the less far the ball travels. Now, I stretch in the morning before I play, I always get to the club half an hour before I have to play, I putt for ten minutes and take a few practice swings. When I'm relaxed, I'll play my best.

It's the same with poker. Eagerness to play will put you off from making an accurate table selection, will disturb your routine of observing your opponents. You'll be focused on your cards, but not on the game as a whole. This is a losing strategy.

Make yourself a mug of tea or coffee, then log on to your site. Spend the time it takes for the coffee to cool and for you to drink it to make your table selection, make yourself comfortable and select a game. Don't buy-in until you've finished drinking, watching the game and noting who is doing what. Then, buy-in, settle down and, calmly, slowly, kill them all.

Notice the Changing Dynamic of Your Game
Switching tables in a card room or casino is tedious enough to put you off from doing so; in a home game, you're well and truly stuck. Online, however, you have complete freedom. You must use this to your benefit.

A game you are consistently beating for the first two hours may change very quickly. The introduction of just one player with a wildly differing style from that of the table may be enough to ruin the game for you. Do not attempt to bully your new adversary off the table, nor believe that one big win by you might see him off. Leave him alone. Games are in constant flux and you must be alert enough to spot when the game goes bad for you. It may be fine for him, he may be having a ball. But, if the early big raises and consistent re-raising doesn't suit you, you must have the courage to log off the table, return to the lobby and make another sensible, informed table selection.

Take a moment or two off, check your healthy bankroll and start a new session. This is a massive advantage of online play, but only if you are disciplined enough to utilise it.

More Chips Should Not Mean More Hands
In a tournament, particularly in its early stages, a big stack allows you to play more hands, hoping to hit a monster. You have enough chips to frighten your opponents that they might go out on the next hand, and you will be playing confidently. The need consistently to obtain more chips is paramount.

In a cash game, you must not be tempted to use a big win

to finance a period of loose play. Whether you are short-stacked or flush, every poor decision costs you profit; you just don't notice it when you have a big stack in front of you. Focus on tightening up after a big win. You can still play your big hands strongly and pick your spots for action but, generally, take a break on anything remotely marginal.

Profit/Loss and Stop/Win Targets

Gamblers who enjoy their hobby know – and usually act upon – the right moment to stop. Many set stop/loss amounts (limiting the amount of profit you can give back to the table) for themselves for each session; others might set targets for the figure they hope to win, and then stop playing.

At poker, you must use your judgment. If you are still playing your best poker and the table conditions are favourable, there is no reason to stop playing.

However, you may wish to lock in some profit. My advice would be to set a figure at which your stop/loss will kick in. At a $1/$2 table, with a $200 buy-in, say, I might decide that once I had doubled my stake (to $400), I would apply a 50 per cent profit/loss. This means that once you have lost 50 per cent of your profit ($100), you will stop play. This ensures that you end your session with a good profit. The down side to this principle is that you may be at a favourable table playing well and you hit a couple of unlucky hands in quick succession. Ultimately, you will develop the insight to judge whether this is the case or whether your play has slipped. In the meantime, the profit/loss scheme will work in your favour.

Never Complain, Never Explain

A good poker player told me this a few years back and it plays in the back of my head whenever I play now. It's the best advice of all.

Online, if you keep that chatbox open, you will be asked questions, abused, and bombarded by the complaints of others. You don't want to see that because it distracts you. You don't want to join in because it distracts you. You turn off the chat box completely.

Hounding Players

Here's a scenario I've seen hundreds of times. There's one player at your table markedly weaker than the rest. Everyone is enjoying snapping at this palooka's chips. He probably re-buys and gets looser. Suddenly, he calls a big all-in bet, way against the odds, and he hits his card. What happens? The idiot who has just been beaten starts to berate the palooka, telling him that he has no idea, no concept of the game, that he's a calling station and a fish. This can go on and on. Sooner or later, the palooka bores of the abuse and leaves – and the table has just lost its most valuable player.

You'll now have angry opponents who will now be harder to read and a new player about whom you know nothing.

You wouldn't ever have been that damn-fool player who hounds a weak player off your table, would you?

Bullying the Short-Stack

Be aware, both in cash games and in tournaments, that short-stacked players have one weapon at their disposal: the all-in re-raise. If you consistently bully the short-stacked player, eventually you will receive this treatment and you may feel you have to call. If you double them up, and lose a stack yourself, you'll feel pretty miserable. Be aggressive against short-stacked players but not indiscriminately: have a hand worth calling the all-in re-raise.

Bully with small raises from which, should the short-stack re-raise all-in, you can escape by making a cheap laydown.

Learning

I play two card games: poker and bridge. The day I think I'm really good at either, I'll give them up. The beauty of both these great games is that they take a lifetime to master, and that mastering them requires study and determination.

If you play golf, you know that while playing 18 holes is more fun, hitting 200 practice shots may improve your game far more.

At poker, it is not just enough to play a lot of hands, you must be focused on them sufficiently to learn from them – win or lose. Particularly while you are in your early-learning stages (this may be after three months or thirty years of poker), it is far more important to improve your game than to win money. Your investment will ensure years of successful, profitable, hugely satisfying poker at the expense of a little short-term adrenalin burst.

To want to win is essential, but to want to learn, to improve as a player, is the ultimate motivation. Naturally, as you improve, you will win. But it must be in that order.

Pick Your Seat

If you are lucky enough to find a choice of seats at the table you have selected, pick one immediately by all means to ensure your place. However, while you are watching the play before buying-in, study your notes on the players and, if necessary, switch seats.

You want the loose and/or aggressive players to your right, where they can bet and raise before you have to act, and the tight and/or passive players to your left so that your raises are respected and your bluffs are likely to run. Having such players to your left also allows you to enter the action with a call, knowing that you will only be raised by premium hands. This tactic would be unavailable to you if you had the constant raiser to your left, as now you would, rightly, be afraid to slip into the action without a very strong hand for fear of bleeding away your bankroll on calls only to fold subsequently to the endless raises.

Physical Health

I'm not trying to act the nanny state here, but your physical health will affect your poker play, both in live games and online. This is why some notable, professional players go to the gym, go running, bring their own friends/masseurs with them to tournaments. Getting some fresh air every couple of hours or so, and resting your eyes, fingers, legs, etc., is vitally important when playing online poker. Simply, you'll feel more alert, and your brain will seem fresher.

If you're hungry, tired or even a little drunk, you're not likely to play your best, and your decisions may not be as smart. Emotion is a factor too. When you're winning, you often feel like you can make any hand you need to win a pot. When you're losing, however, a continued string of beats can seem unbearable. This can lead to tilt and keep you from playing at the top of your game.

Your Opponents' Aims
Clearly, they want to win, don't they?

Because the vast majority of online players are losing players, many of them might want to win, but they will happily settle for not losing. You can use this to your advantage.

Let's say you river the nuts and want to induce your opponent to put more money into the pot. What do you do? The answer depends on many different factors but, ultimately, the question for you is what size bet you think you can get him to call?

One factor to consider is how well your opponent is doing in the game. Is he winning or losing? Let's say you know that a player sat down with $500 and he now has $710. This player is much more likely to call a bet of $140 to $170 on the river than a bet of $220 or $250, because the additional money pushes him into a losing session at your table. For many players, the psychological difference between these two scenarios is huge, even if they don't realise it.

Incidentally, you can use exactly the same thinking when you don't hit your river card and you think that running a bluff may work. Knowledge of bankroll and expectation can often add to the pressure on an opponent to fold to a well-timed bluff.

Quick All-In

As a general, basic rule a quick all-in bet by an opponent suggests weakness, usually a semi-bluff draw.

In higher-level games, this action may be used as a double-bluff, where in fact the player has the best hand but, in low- and medium-stake games, the quick all-in is usually weak.

Betting into Suited Flops

A successful policy in low- and medium-stake games online is to bet when the flop comes suited (i.e: all three cards are the same suit). Often, everyone folds. If there is a call, it may be from a player with the ace of the suit, hoping for the nut flush. A re-raise is usually trips or two pair. When an opponent acts, you can usually judge what to do but, in the meantime, you may have stolen many small pots that did not belong to you.

Betting into Paired Flops

Most poker players do not enjoy seeing a paired flop, since it worries top pair holders and even, in some cases, flush, or flush draw, holders – concerned about trips or full houses. As with the suited flop in low- and medium-stake games, an early bet to the paired flop can often take down the pot there and then.

A call often indicates a draw, or trips; a raise may show top two pair with a confident kicker.

With both of the above situations, if you get action after your bet, unless you feel confident about what you up against, it will be better to go quietly and write off this attempt at a steal.

Flopping Trips

Just a quick reminder that these hands are good, but they are very susceptible to being overtaken by straights and flushes. Online, against more than one opponent, a very big raise should be put in quickly – even a planned check-raise can misfire if your opponent doesn't bet – and against one player, slow playing should be avoided.

The problem with slow plays is that, not only do you sometimes get overtaken, but it is tough to know when to lay down your, formerly, great hand. This means that the risk-reward ratio for slow playing is usually far poorer than we might think. My general advice: flop the trip, bet out quick!

Buddies
Many sites have a button you can click in the note section to indicate that a particular player is a friend or buddy. I don't have buddies online, so I don't use this button for friends. I use it for the players I want to play against: the loose caller, the mad bluffer, the player who thinks he's great but is really very poor. I like, especially, players who are predictably bad. That way I have easy winning decisions to make, and not tough, stressful ones.

Your online poker buddies should be your favourite opponents.

You Lose Quicker Than You Win
This is almost always true, since the profile of a successful player is to win small pots consistently and wait for the occasional big or all-in pot when you have picked your spot and the cards co-operate.

You can't always avoid big pot losses unless you play so tight that you would lose small pots consistently and inevitably get busted session after session.

The key to avoiding the big pot losses is to avoid playing marginal hands and then get tied to them. My all-time least favourite position is one I see online players almost jostling each other to play – the low ace.

Imagine calling an early raise with A5 or A7, or even A10 – whether they are suited or not scarcely makes any difference. What do you want to see hit the flop? An ace? Surely not? Maybe then, you want to see your kicker hit the flop? But, even then, will it necessarily be good? Of course, you will pick up pots playing ace-high poker, but you will also lose big pots when you are out-kickered.

If you must call with a low ace, at least make it suited and never chase the pot unless you can make a cheap or, better still, free draw for the nut flush. However, to call raises, hoping to flop the flush or make a cheap draw, is statistically ridiculous and you will save yourself much money if you respect your opponents' raises and leave calling them for good positions with cards which are easy to play: pairs (great if you trip), suited connectors (well worth playing on if you pick up a straight flush draw).

If you find yourself staring at a premium hand, such as AA, KK, AK, or QQ, then a re-raise will almost always work best, providing further information if your opponent chooses to call or re-raise you.

Raises
I am often asked about raising, and the correct size of raise. In cash games, the standard raise is three and half times the big blind. So, if the blinds are 50/100, a raise to 350 would be the standard action.

If there is already one caller before you have acted, you would make this raise plus a further 100 for the extra player in the hand – so, here, a raise to 450. If there are two callers, you would add on another 100, and make your raise up to 550 – and so on.

As a general rule, if you don't want action after your raise – perhaps with AK, or a low or medium pair – you might raise more (say, X5), and if you did want action because, say, you held AA and there was only one other player in the hand, you might raise less (say, X2.5 the big blind).

Through these raises and their relation to the big blind, you have some opportunity to gauge an opponent's strength. You, yourself, should try to mix up these raises, sometimes raising big with a monster hand (AA, KK) and, maybe raising small with 66 in first position. (It's amazing how often, at an educated table, a small raise in early position will cause the entire table to fold). The important thing is to stick to your default methods most of the time and mix it up a little whenever you have been at the same table, with the same opponents, for any length of time.

When making notes on a player, you should jot down whenever possible the size of his raise, his position and then his hand. Some people in the low- and medium-stake games are remarkably predictable, and, from the size of their raise, easy to read.

In tournament play, the size of raise may also be influenced by the more aggressive nature of the game. In the early stages of the tournament, raises should probably be kept big (perhaps five times the big blind) to avoid too many multi-way pots, which are tough to judge, and also to protect your good hand. Towards the end, when all-in re-raises will be more prevalent, you should opt for smaller raises (X2 or X2.5) so that, if re-raised, you can fold relatively cheaply.

Layers

As well as studying their style of play, it is important to rate each of your opponents in terms of their poker thinking. In low-stake games, or cheap tournament buy-ins, freerolls, etc., this may simply be the cards they are looking at. In higher-stake games and towards the end of bigger tournaments, players are likely to have put you on a hand and have decided what they hope to achieve from the hand. In these situations, you must be aware that your opponent(s) is asking himself questions about your hand, and has established what your hand might be. You must think as he/she does and then think that little bit more deeply. At the highest level of the game, when pros play pros, these layers can go back and forth – through bluff and double-bluff, to triple-bluff and quadruple-bluff and so on. Try to establish how deeply your opponent is thinking – and then think one layer more deeply.

Poker Tracker Software

If you are analytical by nature, you might enjoy purchasing some poker analysis tools. These can be used to provide stats on every hand you have played on any site: analysis as to your success rate defending your blinds, button raising, re-raising, etc., will form a really useful bank of information to help you maximise profitable situations and eliminate long-term money-losing tactics.

Most sites recommend software and there are numerous sites which have reviews of all the available options. Also, ask your friends if they use one type of software – personal recommendation usually being the best kind.

Enjoy Your Game

Above all, enjoy poker. It is a game and it should be enjoyed, even if it takes dedication, determination, study and practice to achieve long-term success. Remember that even the world's greatest players get beaten and make foolish-looking plays.

If you find that you are no longer enjoying your game, stop for a while – maybe a week or a month. You may return refreshed and invigorated, with a more positive outlook and greater knowledge, both of the game and of yourself.

Poker is a gambling game. It can be addictive. Try never to gamble with money you cannot afford. It's easy to do. I, and all my poker-playing friends, have done it at one stage or another. However, playing with "scared money" is a huge handicap, and almost inevitably leads to poor results – and hence, more losses.

Please, if you find that you are losing too much, stop for a while. Talk about it with a good friend, sort out your finances, and play at a level you can afford. However, if you adopt the advice within these pages diligently, and you possess some poker knowledge and skill, this should not be a problem which will affect you often. Be aware, though, that if you move up to higher and higher stakes (it's best to do this very slowly, and only when your bankroll permits) you are likely to go bust from time to time. Even the world's best players are not immune to a terrible run of cards or bad beats.

Unless I am facing you at a big final table, or in a huge cash game – and I hope that I will – I wish you the very best of luck.

GLOSSARY

add-on

in a tournament, you may be offered the opportunity to add to your chips by buying extra chips after the first session of play

all-in

to place all your remaining cards into the pot

ante

bet made before the cards are dealt on each hand

bad beat

a hand where you lose to a player against the expected odds

bet

to make the first movement of chips on any betting round

big blind

the bigger of the two ante bets placed before each hand of Texas Hold 'Em

bluff

to attempt to steal the pot by representing a hand stronger than the one actually held

board   the table; the community cards showing on the table

bubble   the bubble is the position one below the prize-winning positions, and is therefore the least enviable spot in which to be eliminated

burn   to discard; the dealer "burns" the top card before dealing the "flop", "turn" and "river"

button   the dealer button which denotes the position of the dealer; also sometimes referring to the player in that seat

buy-in   the exchange of cash for chips; the amount required to sit at a given table

call   to match the highest bet made to date

cash in   to leave the table and exchange your chips for cash

check   when no other player has bet, to check is to make no bet at that stage (sometimes indicated by tapping the table)

check-raise   a play that is usually strong. To check at first and then, once an opponent bets, to raise him

chip, chips   also known as "checks", these are circular plastic or clay discs which represent different financial values and which are used instead of cash in almost all poker games

community cards   the "flop", "turn" and "river" cards dealt face up in the middle of the table

dealer   the player who deals (or for whom a paid dealer deals) the deck before this honour moves on to the next player in a clockwise direction

dog   short for underdog

double through   a chance to double your chips on one hand (usually by taking a bit of a gamble)

down cards   your "hole" or "pocket" cards

draw   to improve your hand with the community cards

early position   the player positions closest to the left of the dealer; the first players to decide what to do

fifth street   the fifth and final community card, also known as "the river"

final table   the last table of ten players (sometimes eight) in a tournament when all other players have been eliminated

fish   a player who stays in pots hoping to catch the right cards to create a winning hand – but against the odds

flop   the first three community cards

flush   five cards of the same suit

flush draw   when you have four cards of the same suit and you are hoping that the subsequent card(s) will produce a fifth card to complete the flush

fold   to throw away, or muck, one's cards

fourth street   the fourth community card, also known as "the turn"

heads-up   head-to-head play at a table containing only two players

high-roller   a player who competes for very high stakes

hole cards   the player's two secret cards, dealt face down

hole, in the   as above

home game   poker played at home

house, the   the casino or club in which you are playing

kicker   card or cards not involved in the formation of a poker combination, but still part of the five-card poker hand

late position   player(s) closest to the dealer's right, last to act on each round of the betting

lay down   to concede or give in; often a good play in poker if you feel that you are beaten

limp in   to call a small bet in "late position" when you are unlikely to be raised

loose   a loose player is likely to play too many hands, remain in pots for too long and make speculative plays which will result in chips being lost

mid position   in the middle of the table between the big blind and the dealer

muck   to fold or discard

no-limit   a game with no maximum limits on the amount which can be bet

nut, nuts   the best possible hand; a "nut" flush would be an ace-high flush, with no chance of a straight flush

off   unsuited

out, outs   card or cards which will complete your hand and improve it, usually to winning status

overcard   card or cards which are higher than those showing among the community cards

palooka   an inexperienced card player

pocket rockets AA "in the hole"

position   a player's location at the table, measured in terms of the order in which action must be taken on each round of the betting

pot   the collection of chips (sometimes cash) which will be awarded to the winner of the hand

raise increase the size of the biggest bet at the table

re-buy in a tournament, when you lose all your chips early on, you may be offered the opportunity to pay the entry fee again for another chance and another set of starting chips

re-raise as above, once a player has already raised; considered a very strong intimidating move

river the fifth and final community card, sometimes known as "fifth street"

rock a player who chooses only the best hands to enter the action and bets only when he is sure that he is best

rush a roll, a sequence of successful plays

satellite a qualifying event for a big poker tournament

school a regular poker game, acknowledging that you never stop learning; a poker school

set three of a kind, "trips"

short-handed a poker game containing four players or fewer; the value of hands often changes as a result of having fewer players at the table

short-stack when you have less than the average amount of chips in front of you

showdown   when a bet (or bets) is called after the river card, all players must show their hole cards; the best hand wins

side pot   a secondary (sometimes tertiary) pot, formed because one player is all-in and cannot bet any more into the pot, contested by the remaining players

slow play   to give the impression of weakness or uncertainty by checking or calling bets rather than raising them

slow-rolling   to turn over a winning hand slowly after another player believes that he has won; poor form at the poker table

straight   five cards of mixed suits in sequence

Stud, 5-card   an old variation of poker where you are dealt five cards and there is then betting. Not popular these days

suited   of the same suit

super-satellite   a satellite event from which the winner(s) gain a seat in a satellite

tell   an indication, often subconscious or unrecognised by the player himself, by which other players may gain an insight into the strength of a player's hand

tilt, on tilt   usually a sign of frustration or anger, a player may go "on tilt" by playing too many hands of poor quality and subsequently showering opponents with chips

top pair   a pair formed by the highest card on the
                      board and one in your hand

trips   a "set"; three of a kind

turn   the fourth community card, sometimes
                      known as "fourth street"

WSOP   the World Series of Poker – the World
                      Championships of the game, held each
                      summer in Las Vegas

INDEX

To order any Right Way title please fill in the form below

No. of copies	Title	Price	Total
	Texas Hold 'Em Poker: Begin and Win	£5.99	
	For P&P add £2.50 for the first book, £1 for each additional book		
	Grand Total		£

Name: _____

Address:_____

_____ Postcode: _____

Daytime Tel. No./Email_____
(in case of query)

Three ways to pay:
1. Telephone the TBS order line on 01206 255 800.
   Order lines are open Monday – Friday, 8:30am–5:30pm.
2. I enclose a cheque made payable to **TBS Ltd** for £_____
3. Please charge my ☐ Visa ☐ Mastercard ☐ Amex
   ☐ Maestro (issue no. _____)

Card number:_____

Expiry date: _____ Last three digits on back of card:_____

Signature: _____
(your signature is essential when paying by credit or debit card)

**Please return forms to Cash Sales/Direct Mail Dept.,
The Book Service, Colchester Road, Frating Green,
Colchester CO7 7DW.**

Enquiries to readers@constablerobinson.com.

Constable and Robinson Ltd (directly or via its agents)
may mail, email or phone you about promotions or products.

☐ Tick box if you do not want these from us ☐ or our subsidiaries.

**www.right-way.co.uk
www.constablerobinson.com**